THERE AND BACK AGAIN

A decade of travel tales

TIMOTHY IMHOFF

Published By
Cedar Lake Publishing

First Printing: 2015
ISBN: 978-0-9963071-1-6

Cedar Lake Publishing
2392 Cedar Lake Drive
Maryland Heights, Missouri 63043

Book design by Peggy Nehmen at n-kcreative.com
Cover photo by Timothy Imhoff
www.timothyimhoff.com

"*There and Back Again* is a fast-paced series of funny adventure stories from around the world. Timothy Imhoff brings the reader on a memorable ride of bucket-list activities that will have you laughing and adding to your own travel to-do list."

—Pete Williams, Author, *Obstacle Fit*

"Timothy Imhoff's travel memoir, *There and Back Again, A Decade of Travel Tales*, is informative and entertaining. The essential thing about travel memoirs, aside from the actual travel itself, is experiencing such a rapport with the author that his or her experiences feel shared, genuine and dynamic. Imhoff has that gift, and his travel stories are a delight to read."

—Jack Magnus for Readers' Favorite (5-star review)

"Timothy Imhoff has succeeded in writing a humorous, to the point book that is a cute mix of romance and travels with his wife. One can actually see Tim and Rachel's relationship evolve with their shared travel and experiences. Overall, it is a great book that will help you make up your mind about traveling to all those places that you have been dreaming about."

—Dr. Olivia Dsouza for Readers' Favorite (5-star review)

For Rachel

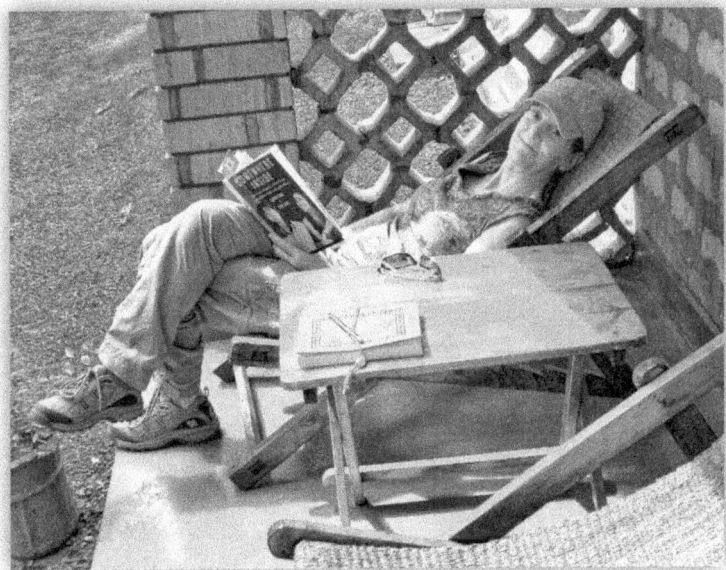

"I own this place. I inherited it from my gram. She ran it as a bookstore for, like, a hundred years. When she passed, she willed it to me. And well, I love books, but I had to jazz things up."

"I think it's wonderful! I've never been in a place quite like it."

"Where are you from? I haven't seen you in before."

"I'm on a summer road trip and just arrived today. I teach at a university in Wisconsin."

Katie silently held Annie's eyes for a moment. "Well, welcome, Professor Annie. I hope you enjoy our town and my establishment."

Annie smiled. "I already am." She looked down and realized that she was still holding Katie's hand. *How odd,* she thought, releasing it. For the third time in the last few days, she felt her pulse racing.

Annie enjoyed an hour or so of people-watching and chatted with Katie a few times between customers. When it was time to take care of her bill, Katie brought over a flyer, advertising live music the next night. "Wednesday nights, we always have live music. There are some really good female musicians in Portsmouth who do acoustic sets. We usually schedule two performers each Wednesday. You should come tomorrow, Annie."

Annie smiled. "I definitely will come by. Thanks for the invite!"

"Cool beans!" Katie said, smiling. "And by the way, your bill has been taken care of."

Annie glanced up and down the bar, a little anxiously. "By who?"

"Well, by your cute bartender, of course!"

Annie looked at Katie and smiled. "Thanks, Katie. That was very sweet of you. I've never heard that expression—'cool beans.' Is that a New Hampshire thing?"

"I guess so. My gram used to say that all the time. So did my mom. Well, music starts at eight tomorrow. I'll see you then."

"See you tomorrow."

Annie enjoyed a leisurely walk back to the inn, replaying her enjoyable evening as she strolled. *What a great start to my trip,* she thought. *And I think I even made a friend.* She was really looking forward to the following night.

Once back in her room, Annie undressed and pulled a large T-shirt out of the dresser drawer. She paused for a moment, put it back, and slipped under the covers naked. "Well, it's the start of an adventure, and I did so enjoy the Naked Lady wine," she said aloud. She laughed quietly and enjoyed the sensations of the clean sheets on her skin.

Annie noticed a journal on the bedside table and picked it up. Inside, she saw that previous guests of the Mountain Laurel Room had written about their experiences in Portsmouth and at the Cranberry Inn. *What the heck,* she thought. *I haven't written in my own journal yet during this trip.* She picked up the pen that had been left beside the guest journal and sat up against the headboard with a pillow propped behind her. She thought for a minute, trying to decide what to share with the people who would stay in the room in coming weeks and months, and then began to write.

This is definitely My Year of Adventure. My husband of several years had an affair this past year. I mourned, cried, begged, and lost a bunch of weight. I even tossed some of his clothes out a window, onto the front lawn. Now I'm living in the now, as they say. I am on my first road trip. I'll see several parts of New Hampshire and Maine. I'm going to paint, hike, and eat and drink anything I want. This is my year. I can't wait to see what tomorrow may bring. Carpe diem!
—Annie from Wisconsin

Annie read her entry and laughed. "They will think I'm a wacko!" She turned off the light, lay back down, and was asleep in no time.

Contents

Preface

In J. R. R. Tolkien's beloved books *The Hobbit* and *The Lord of the Rings*, readers are introduced to a wonderful character, Mr. Bilbo Baggins. Bilbo is, among other things, an aspiring author. The outcome of his writing efforts is a book titled, *There and Back Again—A Hobbit's Tale*. The book is described as capturing many years of expeditions, adventures, danger, and intrigue in the make-believe land of Middle Earth. Tolkien's readers do not actually get to read this book but are certain that it is amazing. I was introduced to Tolkien's books in high school and have read them several times since. They instilled in me a desire for travel and adventure.

I met Rachel Dietz in October 2004. It was an adventurous first date that included a dangerous trek through an adult Halloween costume contest in the Central West End neighborhood of St. Louis. When we were married fourteen months later, our vows promised a life filled with adventures.

Over the last decade, Rachel and I have had many such adventures. Some have been close to home, and some have taken place in distant countries. Some have been a bit dangerous. Many have been very funny. I think that some are even worth sharing! We have learned that our world is filled with diversity and that if we are ready, adventure and romance are just around the corner, even for folks over the age of fifty!

I would like to thank J. R. R., Bilbo, and Rachel for inspiring me to write this book. The first sixteen travel tales are descriptions of actual travel adventures that Rachel and I have shared. They are told to the very best of my recollection, and Rachel helped with some details. The final part of the book is a preview of a new novel, *Painted Wings*. This is an original work of fiction, inspired by one of our true travel tales.

I hope you enjoy the trip!

Acknowledgements

Several people played an important role in helping bring this book to life. Thanks to John Imhoff and Gil Dietz for feedback on the early drafts. Thanks to my editor, Stephanie Ernst, for her support, guidance, and suggestions. Thanks to Peggy Nehmen from N-K Creative, for the beautiful cover design and production ideas.

A special thank you goes to my travel partner and wife, Rachel Dietz, for her encouragement and suggestions. I can't imagine a better partner to share life's adventures. Here's to the next decade!

PART 1
Costa Rica Adventures

1

Bamboozled at the Ferry

Rachel and I planned the details of our trip to Costa Rica in 2005 carefully. Plans included a private wedding on a secluded beach on the Pacific Ocean. Rachel was an experienced traveler, having spent time in Europe, Australia, and South Africa. This was going to be my first trip outside of North America. We made all of the arrangements ourselves and decided to rent a car and drive from destination to destination. The travel guides described the roads in Costa Rica as being pretty rough, with many regions having only gravel and dirt roads.

Our plan was to arrive at the airport in San José in midafternoon, get our rental car (hopefully with all-wheel drive and automatic transmission), and drive west to Puntarenas. In Puntarenas we would catch a car ferry and cross the Gulf of Nicoya to Paquera. From Paquera, we would drive the twenty-five miles or so to Montezuma. The staff at the resort where we were staying assured us that this sounded like a reasonable plan. The travel guides emphasized that there are two ferries that leave Puntarenas from the same location. One goes to Paquera and the other to Playa Naranjo, a town farther north on the Nicoya Peninsula. The road between Playa Naranjo and Paquera was described as one of the worst in the country and one to be avoided.

The flights were smooth and without delay. My first experience going through Customs in a foreign country was exciting, and the lines were not bad. We made the connection with the car rental company in San José and were pleased to see both all-wheel drive and an automatic transmission on our cute little SUV. Rachel and I headed out on Highway 1, one of the only modern highways in the country. The highway was mostly two lanes, with occasional passing lanes on hills. Traffic was heavy with lots of trucks, and the roadsides were congested with pedestrians walking or waiting for buses. We were not making very good time, and it quickly became clear to Rachel and me that there was no way we were going to make the entire trip to Montezuma by nightfall. It was time to come up with a Plan B!

Rachel called the resort to let them know that we would arrive the next day. The resort employee tried to convince Rachel that we should try to make the ferry and the drive, even if it was in the dark. Rachel politely declined and said that we would catch a ferry first thing in the morning. We found a hotel in Puntarenas in one of the tour books we had brought along and called for a reservation. Upon reaching the hotel, we parked the car in a fenced, guarded lot a few blocks from the hotel. From what we had read, Puntarenas had a reputation of being a little rough.

In the hotel lobby we ran into a family from the United States who had a private driver. He recommended a restaurant nearby that had good seafood, and we followed his suggestion. The restaurant was small, the staff friendly, and the food was good. We were glad that we had decided to stop for the night. Back at our room, we watched the activity at a city park just across the street. At nine in the evening, the park was filled with families and couples. People were walking, playing soccer, or just relaxing with a beverage and snack. It seemed very safe and pleasant.

Rachel and I were ready early the next morning; we wanted to get in line right away for the ferry that ran every two hours. We had an appointment mid-morning with the attorney who was going to handle the legal paperwork for our marriage and also perform the ceremony. He lived in a small town, just a few miles from our destination resort. We found the dock and parked the car in a long line of cars and trucks. After we had been waiting for ten minutes or so, a young man wearing a white uniform and carrying a clipboard approached our car. We figured later that he had selected us because we were the only people who looked like US tourists.

"Good morning, my friends!" he said as he gave us a winning smile. "My name is Miguel, and I am here to assist you this morning. You will follow me, and I will get you in a much shorter line for the ferry that will leave very soon. You will be much faster than these old trucks!"

"We want to go to Paquera," I said. "They told us this is the line for the Paquera ferry."

"Oh yes, my friends. I will take you to the correct ferry. It is so. Please get in your car and follow me. The ferry will leave soon, and I must purchase your ticket."

I looked at Rachel. She shrugged her shoulders. "I guess so," she said.

I pulled our car out of line, and followed Miguel as he walked past all of the waiting cars and trucks. We stopped in front of an office, where Miguel asked Rachel for money to buy the ferry ticket. He named a price in *colones*, and she gave him the money. He bought the ticket and then led us to a different ferry that was almost finished with the boarding process. Miguel talked with a crew member, led us onto the ferry, and showed us where to park.

We were the last passengers to board the ferry, and we watched as the crew began to prepare for departure. Miguel approached Rachel, who was standing next to our car. "Thank you very much for your business, señorita!" Miguel said. I was surprised when suddenly he bent down and kissed Rachel right on the lips. He laughed and then jumped over the chain that had been stretched across the back of the ferry and ran down the sidewalk.

"People in Costa Rica sure seem friendly," Rachel said as she wiped her mouth. We both laughed.

As the ferry left the port, Rachel and I calculated the price in US dollars that we had paid for the ticket. We figured out that Miguel had charged us several times what the actual cost of the ticket was. We also realized that the ferry was heading north out of Puntarenas and not south. This meant that our helpful guide had put us on the wrong ferry, and we were heading toward Playa Naranjo, and the trip to Montezuma was going to be much more difficult. We did our best to keep a sense of humor about everything. There wasn't anything we could do but try to get into the spirit of the adventure.

"Just think, Rachel—we get to see a part of Costa Rica that we hadn't planned on seeing," I joked. An hour and a half later, we drove off the ferry in Playa Naranjo. We were a little off course.

The road between Playa Naranjo and Paquera lived up to its reputation. Though the route was only twenty-one miles long, our average speed was about five miles per hour as we swerved to avoid large, sharp rocks in the dirt road and followed hairpin turns and even a few figure eights. It was a little consoling that there was another car following us with a family of tourists making the same trek that we were. I wondered whether they had planned their trek this way or whether they had been bamboozled too. We eventually made our way to Paquera, Tambor, and Cóbano. The attorney worked from his home in Cóbano. Because we had given ourselves plenty of extra time in our schedule, we were nearly on time for our appointment even with the misdirection. Juan Carlos was having breakfast with his wife and four-year-old son when we arrived. He was a young man with black hair and a black beard. He was very friendly and spoke good English.

We took care of the legal paperwork with Juan Carlos and talked about the kind of ceremony we would like. He asked what we would be wearing and let us know that since the ceremony was on the beach, he would probably be barefoot. He said that he liked to talk about nature in these ceremonies. That sounded good to us. Juan Carlos described the different levels of approval that our paperwork would go through, getting numerous stamps from different offices in the Costa Rican government. If all went smoothly, we'd have the official marriage documents mailed to us in a few months. He was very excited that he had just downloaded Google Earth to his computer, and he showed us how he could look up and see a picture of our house in Missouri. He printed a copy to send in with our marriage paperwork.

Rachel and I drove the last few miles from Cóbano to Montezuma feeling more relaxed and excited. Everything had worked out after all. It wasn't the trip that we had planned, but we made it to Montezuma unscathed, and the next day we were going to be married!

On our return trip from Montezuma and the Nicoya Peninsula, fortune was definitely on our side, and our faith in our fellow man was restored. We purchased a ticket for the correct ferry this time, but perhaps I was anxious because of our first ferry trip. After purchasing our ticket and starting to walk away from the counter, I felt someone tap my shoulder. I turned to see a young Costa Rican man smiling at me. He had been in line behind us.

He pointed at the counter. "Dinero," he said.

"Dinero," I said to myself. "Money." I looked past him, and there was my wallet, sitting on the counter where I had set it down. My heart raced. *That could have been a disaster*, I thought.

I picked up the wallet. "Muchas gracias, señor! Muchas gracias!" I said.

Rachel and I both shook his hand, and we all laughed. Rachel and I were glad to experience such a wonderful example of honesty and friendliness between strangers.

"Pura vida," he replied. "Good life." In the next two weeks, we would see that message on billboards all over Costa Rica.

The car ferry crossing the Gulf of Nicoya, Costa Rica, 2005

2

Exchanging Vows on the Sand

After Rachel and I decided to have a private destination wedding, it didn't take long for us to choose Costa Rica as the location. We had both wanted to travel there. It was easy to get flights in and out. Costa Rica was even in the same time zone as St. Louis. We researched different locations and decided on a beach wedding in the town of Montezuma, at the Ylang Ylang Beach Resort. A small beach town at the bottom of the Nicoya Peninsula on the Pacific Ocean, Montezuma has a history of attracting young travelers on a budget and colorful characters. Getting there would involve an interesting drive from the airport in San José, on winding roads of pavement and then gravel and then dirt.

We decided to keep our wedding plans to ourselves and make this a very simple and private affair. We told my young adult children, Dan and Laurel, a few days before we left but did not share our plans with other family, friends, or coworkers. They knew only that we were going on a travel adventure in Costa Rica. We researched the legal requirements for an international marriage and were surprised when St. Louis County officials told us that as long as the marriage was legal in Costa Rica, it would be recognized by the county. The owner of the resort connected us with a local attorney, Juan Carlos, to help with the legal process. In Costa Rica, weddings may also be conducted by an attorney. We arranged to meet him in his office in Cóbano, a neighboring town, the day before the wedding.

Rachel and I enjoyed our secret preparations for the event. We laughed as we discussed how one dresses for a private beach wedding in remote Costa Rica. Rachel quietly shopped for a dress and found a simple but beautiful dress in a beach shop in Florida while on a work trip. I found a white linen shirt at Plowsharing Crafts, a fair trade shop in St. Louis, and bought a new pair of jeans. We both chose sandals since our ceremony would be in the sand.

When we arrived in Montezuma, we checked in at another small hotel owned by the proprietors of the Ylang Ylang Beach Resort, Patricia and Lenny. We parked our car there, and a jeep picked us up with our luggage and drove us down the beach to the Ylang Ylang, which was situated about a mile outside of the small village of Montezuma. There were no roads and no vehicles allowed on or near the property. Walking the beach was the only way to travel. The Ylang Ylang was the perfect romantic getaway. The resort had a total of twelve private accommodations, most of which were round, yellow huts made of natural materials with thatched roofs. The windows were open to the air, without screens or glass. Rachel and I were happy to see that our hut had its own bathroom but were surprised that our bathroom had no door, just a hexagon-shaped opening in the wall. The shower was outside on the side of the hut, with beautiful natural rock and stone for the walls and floor.

The Ylang Ylang had a nice restaurant with outdoor seating only. It was thought to be the best restaurant in town. The wait-staff must have lived on-site or nearby because we were served every morning by Cecilia and every evening by Ramon, two beautiful and friendly local people. One evening we decided to walk into town for dinner, for a change of pace. When we returned, the owner, Patricia, looked at us quizzically and asked why on earth we would choose to eat somewhere else. She was right. Our dinner in town had paled in comparison to what was offered at the Ylang Ylang. The resort also boasted a nice swimming pool with a waterfall.

Our yellow hut was just yards from the beach and the Pacific Ocean. The sound of the surf was soothing for me, but it kept Rachel awake some nights. In the early mornings we were awakened by howler monkeys announcing the beginning of a new day. At night we heard the sounds of animals scurrying by our hut or walking through the dry leaves on the other side of the wall. We frequently saw a beautiful blue and green lizard, at least three feet long from nose to tail, walking down the path to the beach or climbing up the side of a nearby palm tree.

The morning of our wedding was sunny and beautiful. We woke up around six thirty and took a long walk on the deserted beach. I took some great pictures of Rachel in the early morning light. I knew she was going to be a beautiful bride in just a few hours. We had a delicious breakfast and later in the morning walked the beach in the other direction. When we returned to our hut, the sidewalk around it was dusted with rose petals. On the recently made bed was a towel sculpture in the shape of a heart, and more rose petals were sprinkled on the bedspread. It was so romantic!

We relaxed for a few hours and then got dressed for the ceremony mid-afternoon. As I had expected, Rachel was lovely in her simple, elegant white dress. We walked the short distance from our hut to the restaurant to meet Juan Carlos and Patricia. Patricia had volunteered to take some pictures for us. Our favorite waiter, Ramon, greeted us when we arrived. He laughed and told us that he had known someone was getting married that afternoon but was surprised that it was us. I guess we were a little older than the typical bride and groom. Juan Carlos arrived with his wife Carmen and their four-year-old son, Julian. We were going to have a small audience after all. Patricia joined us, bringing Rachel a beautiful bouquet of flowers to carry, picked fresh from the gardens of the resort, and we were ready to begin.

We walked out onto the beach to a spot that Patricia recommended because of the natural light for the pictures. There were a few other people on the beach, but Rachel and I were in our own world by then. We stood facing each other, smiling, with Juan

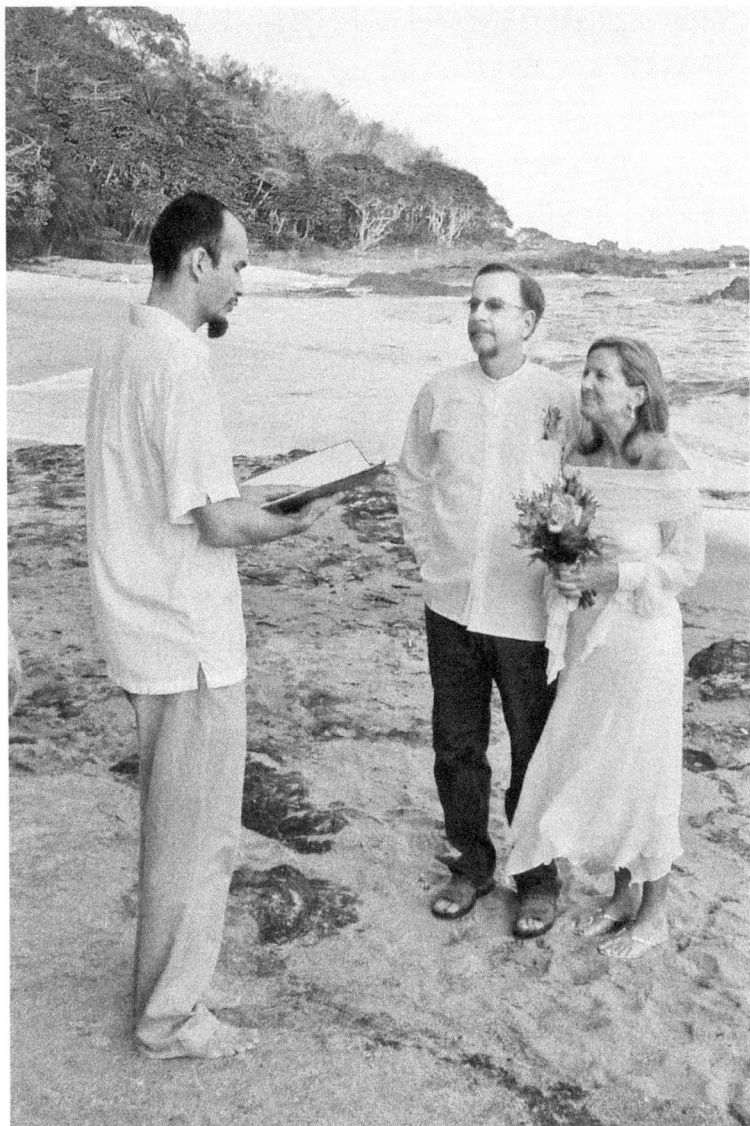

*Our barefoot wedding on the beach, Ylang Ylang Beach Resort,
Montezuma, Costa Rica, 2005*

Carlos forming the third point of the triangle in his simple white shirt and khakis. Patricia quietly moved around us, taking a few pictures. Carmen held Julian and stood a little ways away. The ceremony was simple. Juan Carlos invoked images of nature in his introduction, talking about the sun, wind, and stars. We each shared the vows that we had written. Rachel had memorized hers. I read mine from a small sheet of paper. When we placed our silver rings on each other's fingers, Rachel put mine on my right hand instead of my left, and I had trouble taking it off to switch it to the other hand. Juan Carlos laughed and told me to relax—it would be just fine. We all got a laugh out of the moment, and within a few minutes we were married!

We walked down the beach for a few more pictures and then returned to the patio of the restaurant. We had purchased special champagne on a trip to Napa in California. It was waiting for us on the patio, on a table decorated with beautiful flowers. We enjoyed a glass with Juan Carlos, Carmen, and Patricia, as Julian played with his toy car on the patio floor. We invited Ramon to join us as well. He was surprised and pleased to be included.

A second table for two was set up at the end of the patio. A beautiful floral arrangement was at the center of the table, and several candles surrounded it. We had a romantic candlelit dinner that evening at our table on the beach. The rest of the diners were separated from us, giving us a bit of privacy. But we laughed as they kept glancing our way, smiling at the newlyweds.

Our day was just what we had hoped it would be!

3

Close Encounters of the Primate Kind

The rain forests of Costa Rica are rich in their variety of birds and other animals. Since the places where Rachel and I stayed were often nestled close to the beach or jungle, we felt like we were sharing the natural environment with the creatures that lived there, including the little lizards that visited through the unscreened windows and the large one that woke us up at night walking through the dry leaves just behind where we were sleeping.

"Do you think he is inside or outside, Tim?"

"Oh, I'm sure he's outside. Go back to sleep."

"Could you check and make sure?"

"Sure, sweetie. Anything for you!"

Then there was the large brown beetle that resembled a five-inch cockroach that we found inside one morning and the army of large white ants that invaded my suitcase when I left it open one day. Two of the more exciting encounters were with primates, the howler monkeys and the white-faced capuchin monkeys.

The howler monkeys were our alarm clock most mornings in Montezuma. Howlers are one of the largest of the world's monkeys, and they have a spooky, deep guttural growl or howl. They sounded like gorillas hooting as they beat their chests. Howlers are thought to be one of the loudest land animals, and their vocalizations can be heard for miles. When we were in bed in our small hut at the Ylang Ylang, the howlers sounded like they were in the trees just above us. We never saw a howler in the flesh—they are shy and prefer to avoid human contact—but they sure let us know that they were around. During one early morning beach walk, we encountered an area of trees that had at least two howlers announcing the coming of the new day. I walked into the trees looking for them but was unsuccessful. Rachel preferred to stay a distance away. I assured her that their bark was probably worse than their bite!

Our second primate encounter was much more dramatic. A day or two after our beach wedding, we drove to the Cabo Blanco Absolute Nature Preserve, a few miles out of Montezuma. Our plan was to do some hiking, take some pictures, and walk on the beach. We checked in at the office at the entrance to the park and picked up a map of the park and trails. The young woman behind the counter was friendly and wished us a fun day. We found the trailhead and entered the jungle. The trail was wide and easy to follow. About fifteen minutes into our hike, we heard noises coming from high in the trees above us. Looking up, we spotted a white-faced capuchin monkey jumping from branch to branch. Rachel and I were excited and began trying to get his picture. Unfortunately, he was quite excited as well. Soon he was screeching in an agitated way and ripping small branches off of the trees. Suddenly, it felt like it had begun to rain a little, but it was a clear, sunny morning. "I think he's trying to pee on us," Rachel said. We decided to move on.

As we walked down the trail, we continued to see white-faced monkeys in the trees above us, and we continued to stop and take pictures. We even saw several females carrying babies. We were feeling lucky. Then the screeching, branch ripping, and agitation started again. But this time there were lots of white-faced monkeys in the trees above us. We had entered their encampment. We began to feel a little uncomfortable. A few of the monkeys started shaking the branches of the palm trees they were in, hundreds of feet above our heads. Coconuts began to fall around us, big coconuts! They were falling from so high up that they sounded like bombs going off when they hit the ground. "Do you think they are doing that on purpose," I asked, "like trying to hit us?"

"I'm not sure, but I think we ought to get out of here," Rachel replied.

We decided it was time to get moving. At least they were high up in the trees, I thought. They must have read my mind because a few of the monkeys then ran down the trunks of the palm trees, jumped onto the path in front of us, and showed us their teeth. They looked like big, sharp teeth. It was definitely time to get away from their territory. We weren't quite sure whether to go forward or retreat, but the forward path led to our destination, so that's the one we took. We made it out of the monkeys' area without further incident and arrived at a road leading to the beach. Along the road was a religious shrine with a statue of St. Francis, patron saint of animals. We stopped and said thank you to him for helping us make it through safely! When we made it back to the place where we had checked in, there were a few very tame white-faced monkeys hanging around and begging for snacks. We kept our distance!

Later we would learn that white-faced capuchin monkeys are among the most intelligent of the primates, and they live in groups of up to forty individuals. They are noted for their use of tools for food gathering and as weapons (their use coconuts, for example!). They are famous for being highly aggressive, and killings are a common occurrence. Males kill other competing males and also infants, in order to stop the mother from nursing, thereby improving breeding opportunities. Troops kill other monkeys that travel into their territories.

Rachel and I laughed at the prospect of a specialist in traumatic brain injury receiving his brain injury as the result of a coconut assault by a monkey in Costa Rica.

A frequent visitor to our honeymoon cottage: a three-foot lizard,
Ylang Ylang Beach Resort, Montezuma, Costa Rica, 2005

4

A Room with a View

A few days after our wedding in Montezuma, Costa Rica, Rachel and I set off to find the Arenal Volcano in the north central region of the country. We had read that the number of people who have seen an active volcano in person is less than one in a million.

Arenal is Costa Rica's most active volcano. It rumbles and spews lava and lava rocks most every day and night. The question on our visit was how much would be visible, since the Arenal Volcano borders an area of cloud forests and rain forests. It is not far from the Monteverde Biological Cloud Forest Reserve. But make no mistake: Arenal is for real. Hikers are prohibited from climbing the volcano, and hikers ignoring that warning have been killed as recently as 2000. The last major eruption was in July 1968. The magnitude of the eruption surprised both scientists and local residents. The nearby village of Tabacon was wiped out, and eighty people were killed.

After our adventurous drive from San José to Montezuma, Rachel and I felt more comfortable driving, and the trip to the Arenal region went without any significant difficulties. We were stopped by the police at one roadblock. The travel books had warned us about these stops and had reported that sometimes they were scams, with uniformed personnel looking for bribes. The guide books suggested just not stopping and instead driving to the nearest police station to make sure that the personnel were legitimate. That was great advice unless you were looking at a group of heavily armed guys, successfully stopping every car on the road. The individuals manning our roadblock were waving every other car through and searching only the other half. Fortunately, we ended up in the half being waved through.

We made it across the Gulf of Nicoya on the correct car ferry and found our way to La Fortuna and the Arenal area. It was a sunny afternoon when we arrived, and as we came around a curve on the highway, there it was: the volcano was a large, perfectly shaped cone. It looked massive. The top of the cone was surrounded by a few swirling clouds. Whether they were regular clouds or steam from the lava, we weren't sure. But the sight was beautiful, and we stopped on the road to take a few pictures. We were glad later that we did because that was the only time the entire volcano was visible during the days we were there.

Our destination was the Arenal Observatory Lodge. This is the closest lodging to the volcano and is located within the national park. The Arenal Observatory used to be a scientific observatory run by the Smithsonian Institution. In the late eighties, it was transformed into the lodge. Travel books recommended having a four-wheel-drive vehicle to make it up the five-and-a-half-mile dirt road to the lodge. Our little SUV came with all-wheel drive, and we negotiated the road without a problem. The Arenal Observatory Lodge was located on a large and beautiful campus. The landscaping of native flowering bushes and plants was striking, and over the two days we saw many different animals scampering between the jungle and the grounds. Some we recognized, and some we did not.

Our room was like nothing we had experienced before. The room itself was quite simple, with a double bed, a dresser, and a small bathroom. What was surprising was that half of one entire wall was a giant picture window, facing the volcano. When we lay in bed with our pillows propped against the headboard, we had a perfect view of the volcano.

As we looked out, we could see smoke trails running down the sides of the volcano. Every few seconds, a new trail would start, and we'd watch it course down one of the sides. We walked outside to watch and were able to clearly hear the explosions. The volcano was shooting lava rocks into the air from the top of the cone. Following each explosion, the rocks would then rumble down the sides of the volcano, creating the smoky trails. They looked and sounded like small avalanches. Rachel and I watched the lava rocks for an hour or more, wondering how close they sometimes came to the lodge.

The lodge had a nice restaurant, and Rachel and I enjoyed a good meal before heading back to our room. We had arranged for a guided hike early the next morning. It was dark when we returned to our room, and we were amazed by the show that was there for us to enjoy. During the day, the lava rocks had created interesting smoke trails. At night the explosions and trails showed up in bright oranges and reds. We spent a couple of hours watching the lava rocks coming down the volcano and trying to capture the sight on camera. Everything moved so fast that it was challenging to time the shots right. But Rachel succeeded in getting some great pictures of the Arenal Volcano in action! We had read ahead of time in descriptions of the lodge that guests had a hard time getting to sleep because of the never-ending views from each room. That was the case for Rachel and me. How do you just close your eyes and try to ignore an active volcano right outside your window?

The next morning, we joined a group of ten other guests for a hike around the bottom of the Arenal Volcano. Our guide, Roberto, was well versed in the science of the volcano and the history of the region. He identified plants, birds, and other animals that we encountered and led us up to the base of the volcano. We saw areas that had been destroyed in the 1968 eruption. The explosions and smoke trails from the lava rocks were even more powerful as we hiked closer to the bottom of the cone, and we were able to take some spectacular pictures.

That afternoon, Rachel and I visited a place where we could soak in naturally heated thermal springs. I guess all of that heat generated by the volcano has to be used for something! As we lay back in our private natural pool, we marveled at the trip and the day. Not many people have had the opportunity to see an active volcano. This was definitely one of the highlights of our first Costa Rica adventure!

*Our guide goes over precautions before our hike
to the base of the Arenal Volcano, Costa Rica, 2005.*

5

The Headless Quetzal

Three years after our wedding on the beach in Costa Rica, Rachel and I decided to celebrate our anniversary back at the Ylang Ylang Beach Resort. We were curious about whether the roads and travel had improved in the intervening years. On this trip we spent our first night near the airport at a beautiful place called the Vista del Valle. This small resort sat on the edge of a mountainous nature preserve and was the perfect setting in which to rest after traveling and prepare for our next morning's travel. The sign outside of our little hut identified our quarters as "The Mona Lisa."

Rachel and I made sure to get on the correct car ferry in Puntarenas and made it to the Ylang Ylang without incident. We had a few relaxing days on the beach and a surprise romantic dinner on our anniversary, arranged by the owner, Patricia, and the friendly waitstaff.

Our third stop on this trip would be the Monteverde Biological Cloud Forest Reserve. This natural park is a lush, higher-elevation rain forest where guests are able to choose from a variety of guided hiking treks. The star of the possible animal sightings is the quetzal, a colorful bird that has become endangered because of habitat destruction. The quetzal has bright green wings and a ruby-red breast, and males can have tail feathers that reach two feet in length.

Rachel and I had done our research regarding the drive between Montezuma and Monteverde. The guidebooks described the roads as challenging. The second half of the route would take us on gravel and dirt roads winding up into the mountains. The turnoff from the main highway was reported to be unmarked and difficult to locate.

Rachel and I left Montezuma early, giving ourselves plenty of time to make the drive to Monteverde. But there is a saying about the best-laid plans! We were traveling in Costa Rica, after all. We made good time initially and even found the main turnoff from the Inter-American Highway for Monteverde. We drove for about a quarter of a mile before encountering a very basic Costa Rican roadblock. An old red pickup truck was parked across both lanes of the road. An elderly gentleman was sitting on the tailgate of the truck. He stood and approached us when we stopped. The old man did not speak English. He communicated in Spanish and with gestures that the road was closed, and we would need to continue down the highway to find the alternate turnoff for Monteverde.

"Well, we've been down this road before," I said to Rachel.

She laughed. "Just go with the flow, Tim. This is part of the adventure."

I laughed too. One of the things that we had discovered about each other during the past three years was that we were both good travelers and were able to adapt to these kinds of bumps on the road.

We returned to the Inter-American Highway and followed it for several miles, looking for some kind of signage for the alternate turnoff to Monteverde. We did not find any signs and didn't think we had passed any roads that looked substantial enough to be our alternate route. We decided to stop and ask for help with directions at a small *soda*, the Costa Rican term for a roadside store and café. We approached the counter and asked in English whether anyone could help us with directions to Monteverde. The man behind the counter gestured for us to wait and called to the back of the café, "Papi, Papi!"

A very old man hobbled over to us using a cane. He told us he was the only one in the place who spoke a little English. We got out our map and laid it on the counter. He ignored it and began giving us verbal instructions, in a mix of English and Spanish. We were to drive into town, turn left by the gas station, travel for a mile or so, and then turn right past the *biblioteca*. I knew that word meant "library."

Rachel decided to order something to eat and asked for a salad. The man at the counter looked confused and shook his head. Rachel pointed at lettuce and tomatoes behind him. It seemed they were used as ingredients in various dishes, but not as salad fixings. The man reluctantly put a pile of lettuce and a few tomato pieces on a paper plate and looked at Rachel like she was crazy.

We were pleasantly surprised when the directions from Papi turned out to be right on target. We made the correct turns in the little town and were on the road to Monteverde. No wonder others had described the route as poorly marked. It was not a simple turnoff from the main highway. We drove for several miles, and as promised, the road turned from paved to dirt and gravel. The elevation steadily increased as the road wound up into the mountains. In many places there was room for only one vehicle, as the road made sharp turns.

We came around one such turn in the road and saw a long line of vehicles, heading the same direction as us, parked on the side of the road. Most were older pickup trucks and dilapidated cars. The drivers were mostly out of their vehicles, smoking and talking to other drivers. Since the road was quite narrow and had no shoulders, they were parked across a portion of the road. I didn't know what was going on, and I began to pass the last vehicle in the line. The driver gestured for me to stop and to get in line behind him. He wasn't angry. He was just trying to communicate that no one was getting by up ahead. I parked behind him, and Rachel and I got out to see what was happening.

We walked up closer to the front of the line of parked cars and trucks and saw the cause of the delay. A large tanker truck had failed to negotiate a curve and was lying on its side, blocking the entire road. A few navy-blue pickup trucks with blue flashing lights on top were gathered near the accident. They looked like pretty old trucks. As we watched, a number of men in white shirts and dark pants walked back and forth between the overturned truck and their vehicles, talking to each other and pointing to the tanker truck.

"They sort of remind me of the Keystone Kops," Rachel said.

I laughed. "I think you are right. I hope somebody knows what they are doing!"

We saw what looked like gasoline pooling in the ditch next to the road. We were concerned that there were people smoking nearby.

With our navigation delays, we were already cutting it close if we hoped to arrive at our hotel in Monteverde before dark. The prospect of traveling on the small, dirt, mountain roads in the dark, especially while unfamiliar with landmarks and turnoffs, was a little scary. Rachel and I were anxious that we could be stuck on the side of the road for hours, maybe days! After about an hour, a large tow truck arrived and slowly made its way to the overturned tanker. The tow truck operators hitched strong cables to the tanker and proceeded to drag it down the road, on its side, until they reached a wider section of the road. This permitted other vehicles to carefully pass the tanker, one at a time. Since the line extended in both directions, drivers on either side took turns: one vehicle passed the truck going down the mountain, and the next passed going up, and so on. We could not imagine the work that it would take to turn the tanker upright and get it all the way back to a town.

It was dark when we arrived in Monteverde, but we found our hotel. It was called the Sapo Dorado, which means Golden Toad, a species that used to be found in the cloud rain forest around Monteverde but that is now thought to be extinct. When we checked in, we discovered that the young woman in the office did not speak English. I began to ask her something, and she replied, "The phone is in your room."

We assumed she meant that if we called from our room, someone who spoke some English would answer.

When we settled in our room, I called the front desk to ask about where we could eat. Because of our delays, it was getting late. The same young woman answered the phone.

"Hi, this is the man who just checked in to room six."

"The phone is in your room."

"We were wondering if you have food or a restaurant."

"The phone is in your room," she repeated, a little louder this time.

"I know. We are talking on the phone. Is there a good restaurant we could walk to?"

"The phone is in your room!" she shouted.

I said thank you, and Rachel and I decided to walk down to the main street of the town and explore a little. It had started to rain, but the evening was still pleasant. As we walked down the road from the Sapo Dorado, we passed a woman carrying

*An oil tanker blocking the only small road
to Monteverde, Costa Rica, 2008*

a covered dish of food. She stopped us and asked if we had just checked in at the hotel. She was the manager, Maria, and had been expecting us, she explained. Maria gave us a recommendation for a good place for dinner.

The next morning, we were up early for our first hike in the cloud rain forest. We joined a group of four other hikers and were assigned to a wonderful guide named Hector. We spent several hours walking up and down mountain trails as Hector told us about the animals, plants, and history of the reserve and of the town of Monteverde. He said that he had lived there all of his life and that he very rarely left the mountain. Everything that he needed for his family and for himself could be found in this small town on the side of the mountain. Hector reminded me of a very good middle school science teacher I had when I was young.

There were two highlights of that first hike in the cloud rain forest. We were walking on a path with a natural stone wall on the right side, which was covered with two-to three-inch holes. Hector got out a flashlight and invited us to look into one of the holes. Sitting at the bottom of the hole we inspected, a few inches from the entrance, was a medium-sized, hairy tarantula. We were walking through a tarantula city! Rachel even got a good picture of a tarantula watching us from his home in the stone wall.

Later in the morning we passed another guide and his group of hikers. He let Hector know that he thought they had heard a quetzal a ways down the trail. Hector said that it had been a few weeks since he had seen a quetzal during a hike, and he took out several groups each day. Everyone kept a lookout for flashes of color, and after a half hour or so, Hector spotted our quetzal. He set up his large, single-lens binoculars on a tripod, and everyone took a look. The quetzal was as described in the guide books, and the bird's bright colors were striking. It was a male with long red tail feathers. Hector reminded us that quetzals were endangered and that there were only a few left in this region of Costa Rica. We felt very lucky.

Hector showed us how to take a picture with our camera through his binoculars, and Rachel was able to take one before the quetzal flew off. When we looked at the picture later, we saw that at the last minute, the quetzal had turned away from us. But we had captured his beautiful colors, and he was centered pretty well. We had a lovely picture of a headless quetzal. It still is one of our favorite pictures from Costa Rica and hangs proudly in our home.

Headless Quetzal

PART 2
Africa Adventures

6

Musings of a Mzungu Traveling in Sub-Saharan Africa

In early 2012, Rachel and I spent a few weeks traveling with my son Dan in Uganda and Rwanda. Dan was in his second year as a Peace Corps volunteer and was living in the town of Ishaka, Uganda. In a reversal of roles, Dan was our guide for the trip, having mastered Ugandan travel, communication, and negotiation skills. "Dad, when we find ourselves in any negotiation situation about prices or whatever, try to leave the room," he said. "They'll see you coming a mile away and charge us way more than they should."

What follows are a few of the observations and reflections that Rachel and I had about this trip of a lifetime. They are presented in no particular order.

Mzungus

Everywhere we traveled in Uganda, we heard people referring to us as *mzungu*. Dan had told us about this ahead of time, so we were expecting the label. The literal translation of *mzungu* is something like "traveler from far away" or "wanderer." The way it was being used by the people we encountered was more like "white tourist," to put it politely. When we drove through villages and towns, kids would point at us and our van and yell, "Mzungu! Mzungu!" Rachel and I thought that was cute. When we completed our mountain gorilla trekking adventure in Rwanda, we purchased a celebratory T-shirt that said "Mzungu in the Mist" on the back.

At other times when we were walking in a town, we would encounter groups of young men who would watch us and mutter "mzungu" under their breath as we passed. Those interactions did not feel so comfortable and had a threatening sort of feeling. Dan particularly disliked the label and would mutter back at them. He equated the term with the n-word used to label African American people in the United States. There were entire days on the trip when we did not see any other mzungus, so we did sort of stand out.

Children

Uganda has lots and lots of children. It is reported to be experiencing a population explosion. There were children everywhere when we visited. Driving along the roads was like trying to drive on a school playground. The roads were lined on both sides by children walking to and from school. All the kids from a given school wore uniforms made from the same colorful fabric, shirts for the boys and dresses for the girls. We could tell when we

Schoolgirls walking home, Masindi, Uganda, 2012

transitioned from one school's territory to the next because the colors would change. The roads were mostly dirt roads, and the kids were walking barefoot. Both boys and girls had their hair cut very short, so the clothes helped us identify the gender of the kids. We passed a school one afternoon where there were hundreds of kids sitting on the grass outside the school building, listening to a teacher's lesson. One of our favorite memories from the trip was walking through small villages and having small children run up to us, yelling, "Hullo, hullo, mzungu! Hullo!"

Dan's experience at the hospital in Ishaka was that Ugandan parents looked at large families as a sign of prosperity and something to strive for. Incomes were generally low, and more children increased the likelihood that there would be someone to help support parents as they aged. I had read that until recently, the government had reinforced this idea, encouraging parents to have large families. It was common for Ugandan mothers to have seven or more children. We saw several billboards along the highways promoting the concept of smaller family sizes. One posed the question of where the jobs would come from for all of these kids. Estimates indicate that Uganda's population could increase from around 35 million people currently to over 47 million by 2025.

T-Shirts

Do you ever wonder where your old T-shirts end up when you put them in a donation drop box? They end up in Africa, that's where. We saw men, women, and children wearing a tremendous variety of T-shirts with American graphics on them: shirts with the logos of American colleges and universities, shirts for all kinds of fundraisers, shirts for runs and races, shirts with silly slogans, shirts with somewhat naughty messages. Two of our favorite instances were the teenage boy wearing a St. Louis Cardinals T-shirt that even had "Pujols 5" printed on the back and the three-year-old girl wearing a pink hooded sweatshirt celebrating the fiftieth anniversary of *Playboy* magazine.

Rachel and I watched a movie recently called *The Good Lie,* in which Reese Witherspoon plays a vocational counselor who helps four siblings from Sudan get jobs in Kansas City. When they learn that they will be coming to the United States, one girl tells her brother that in the United States maybe they can find out what the slogan on the front of his T-shirt means. His only shirt is a black Nike T-shirt with the Nike swoosh and the "just do it" message.

We noticed that some people were dressed up in fancy clothes at surprising times or places. Across Uganda, the people who pumped our gas at service stations were all women dressed in business suits. It made the job look like something very professional. While visiting Kigali, Rwanda, Rachel and I observed a large number of beggars. Some had disabilities, and some just looked impoverished. Many had babies or small children. A young woman in a wheelchair stood out from the rest because she was dressed in a shimmery blue, floor-length cocktail dress. This was not the attire one would expect for someone begging on the street, but there was a certain dignity about her.

Safety and Security

Rachel and I did not have many experiences in Africa where we felt a serious concern for our safety. But some of the roads were very bad, some of the taxi drivers were a little crazy, and we were forced to ride on the back of motorcycles a few times without helmets because that was the only transport available.

We experienced feelings of unease sometimes regarding either our location or the history of the place we were visiting. When Rachel and I flew into Uganda, our plane first stopped in Kigali, Rwanda, before going on to Entebbe. Staring out the plane's window late at night, we could not help thinking of the recent history of the two countries, the corruption at the highest levels of government, the violence, the suffering, even the genocide. We had watched a few movies that depicted these events in the weeks before our trip. This was not history from hundreds of years ago. These events had happened in the not-distant past.

Rachel and I were aware that some of the conflict and danger continued to this day, in areas close to some of our destinations. We drove past a United Nations refugee camp for people fleeing from the Democratic Republic of the Congo. The borders of Uganda, Rwanda, and the Democratic Republic of the Congo come together in the Virunga Mountains. We would be hiking in these mountains on the Rwandan side, to do our mountain gorilla trek. On that trek we were accompanied by a guard carrying an automatic weapon. Our guide informed us that he was there to protect us from any large animals that we might encounter on the trek, but Rachel and I wondered whether he also was protecting us from bad guys who might cross the border from the Congo, which was close by.

We woke up one morning at our hotel in Kasese, near the Queen Elizabeth National Park, to find the entire hotel looking like an army camp, with soldiers with automatic weapons running around everywhere. The general in charge was an imposing, impressive figure. It turned out that Yoweri Museveni, the president of Uganda, would be giving a speech and staying at the hotel the next night, and the soldiers were securing the area. President Museveni has played an important role in Uganda's history and continues to be a controversial leader who elicits strong feelings from both allies and adversaries. Rachel, Dan, and I were glad when we drove away from the hotel after breakfast.

In Kigali, Rachel and I visited the main memorial to the victims of the Rwandan genocide, which occurred in the spring and summer of 1994, just eighteen years before our visit. Over about one hundred days, hundreds of thousands of people were murdered. At the site of the memorial, thousands of people were buried, and we saw actual remains and many moving photos and stories.

We were struck by how only a few years had passed since this horrific time and by how far the country had come in just a few years to rebuild and reconcile. We had a hard time imagining the leadership that would be required to rebuild such a divided country. Kigali was the most modern city that we visited on our trip, and it looked much like any medium-to-large city in the United States. It had busy sidewalks, office buildings, stoplights, restaurants, and lots of shopping. We had lunch at the actual hotel depicted in the movie *Hotel Rwanda*, the Hôtel des Mille Collines. The images from the movie were vivid in our minds as we sat quietly in this elegant hotel that had helped save the lives of hundreds of Tutsi people just a few years before. As we watched waiters and guests, we wondered which people were Hutu and which were Tutsi and how the reconciliation felt from the inside. We wondered what stories each would tell about their life and experiences during the genocide period.

Lodging and Amenities

When we began making arrangements for our Africa trip, we tried working with a travel company within Uganda. The very pleasant representatives insisted on booking only five-star resorts and calculating a very expensive per-person price for the entire trip, rather than breaking down costs of lodging, vehicles, drivers, meals, and other expenses. After discussions with Dan, we decided to try to make all of the arrangements ourselves. Rachel and I would make reservations at hotels for each destination, and Dan would make arrangements for vehicles and drivers. We were able to find more moderately priced hotels with decent reviews, but we knew that this was going to be an adventure.

Our first night in Uganda was the perfect introduction to Ugandan lodging. We were met at the Entebbe airport by Nelson, our friendly driver from the Boma Guest House. It was dark when we arrived. As we pulled into the parking area for the guest house, Nelson asked, "Where you come from, is the electricity turned on all of the time?" We responded that generally, yes, we had electricity all of the time. In a cheerful voice Nelson told us, "At the Boma Guest House we have frequent power outages, and in fact, there is no electricity this evening."

The walkways were lit by candlelight lamps, as was the registration area. It was really quite beautiful. At check-in we were told, "While the power is out, the bar is open!" Rachel and I did find the bar and had a nice glass of wine while watching the reflection of candles on the water of the pool.

We had that kind of experience at several of the hotels where we stayed. We checked into the Masindi Hotel in the early afternoon. Once in our room, we discovered that there was no power. We walked back to the front desk and talked with the young woman who had checked us in. She told us not to worry. "The hotel has a very powerful generator. We will turn it on once it gets dark. Until then, well, maybe it will come back on, on its own."

Bathroom facilities were a similar adventure. All of the hotels where we stayed had private bathrooms. That was one of our criteria. However, that did not guarantee that the toilet would flush or that the shower would provide warm water. After a few days, we got used to those kinds of inconsistencies. Any kind of private bath seemed luxurious compared to the typical pit toilet that we encountered on the road or at some restaurants. At these facilities there was a hole in the wooden floor. That's all. Some even had the outline of two feet painted on the floor around the hole to illustrate where to stand or squat. No toilet paper was provided, and there was no water to wash hands after.

All of the hotels where we stayed had some kind of restaurant. We were pleasantly surprised to see the variety of menu choices. Breakfast was usually simple, with toast, eggs, coffee, and fruit juice. Many of the restaurants offered both Western and Indian items. I would recommend staying away from the "assorted chicken parts." I tried that for lunch one day, and whatever the mysterious parts were, they did not agree with me.

We stopped at a few of the five-star resorts as we traveled for a cold beverage or a bite to eat. They looked as fancy as any resort in the United States, with prices that corresponded. We were happy with the arrangements that we had made ourselves and felt like we were much more in touch with the communities that we were in, staying in smaller hotels right in the heart of town.

One Million Shillings

Imagine walking up to your local ATM machine and typing in the number 1,000,000. As I write this, the exchange rate between Uganda's currency, the shilling, and the US dollar is one Uganda shilling for 0.00037 US dollars. The first few times Rachel and I stopped at an ATM machine in Uganda, we withdrew a few hundred thousand shillings. We were surprised when after buying gas, lunch, and a few odds and ends, we were already low on cash. Dan suggested that we start withdrawing in increments of one million shillings. Fortunately, currency came in large enough denominations that we did not need a wheelbarrow to carry all of the cash. That was a weird experience! It did amaze us that ATM machines were easy to find in any town we visited and that our debit card from our local bank in Missouri worked just fine. We had informed our bank and credit card companies that we would be traveling in Africa, so that they wouldn't be surprised and freeze our accounts.

The other technology that we were impressed with was cell phones. Uganda and Rwanda are very poor countries. Many people do not own cars. Many people live in huts without electricity or running water. Subsistence agriculture is a major way of life. But it seemed like most people carried cell phones. Small shops that sold cell phone cards to pay for minutes were everywhere. At a colorful market I took a picture of a beautiful woman sitting on the ground, surrounded by vegetables that she was selling. It looked like a scene that could have taken place hundreds of years ago. When I looked at the picture later, I realized that she was holding a cell phone and probably texting someone!

How Much Stuff Can You Balance on Top of Your Head?

It looked like walking was the primary mode of transportation for the majority of people we saw. The roads and highways were crowded with people walking and others pushing bicycles—not riding bicycles, but pushing them. In order to transport stuff, people had to carry it, one way or the other. The most interesting were the people balancing an incredible amount and variety of things on top of their heads. I took a great picture of a woman walking down the street in Jinja with a huge basket of bananas on her head. But anyone can carry a basket of bananas! We saw people balancing stacks of pots and pans on their heads. There were men balancing construction materials on their heads, even pallets of bricks. Many families heat their homes and cook with charcoal, so we saw many people with huge bundles of charcoal or wood on top of their heads.

Bicycles allowed people to carry even more stuff. In some cases, it looked like the belongings of a whole house had been lashed to the bike. Other people had half of a farmers' market attached to their bikes. One of the staples of Ugandan cuisine is *matooke*, boiled and mashed green bananas. We frequently saw bicycles loaded down with hundreds of bunches of green bananas. We took pictures of many of these sights.

A woman with a basket of bananas, Jinja, Uganda, 2012

7

Nurses, Tailors, Elephants, and Honeybees: Peace Corps Adventures in Uganda

In our travels with Dan around Uganda, Rachel and I had the opportunity to meet several different Peace Corps volunteers working in the country. Many had joined at the same time as Dan for their two-year assignment. We listened as they shared their successes, challenges, and funny stories. All had interesting experiences to share.

The Peace Corps has an unusual operating model for its mostly young adult volunteers. Each volunteer is assigned to a town and is given a local contact person. The organization the volunteer will work with is responsible for helping find his or her housing. The volunteer is responsible for conducting a needs assessment in his or her community and then coming up with the projects that will be done over the volunteer's two years of service. The projects might have a focus on education, health care, agriculture, or some other area. Volunteers are expected to do their project with no funding from the Peace Corps, other than a small stipend for living expenses. Rachel and I both thought that this would be very challenging, especially for a young adult with not a lot of life or work experience.

Since numerous volunteers complete their service every year, Rachel and I thought that it would be more effective to assign some volunteers to continue good projects that had been started by previous volunteers. But that did not seem to be the usual way of doing things. I read the blogs of many volunteers and met several more, and it seemed like about half of the volunteers came up with valuable projects, and the other half struggled to find a way of really making an impact over their two years of service. Those were the volunteers who seemed to have the least satisfaction with their experience in the Peace Corps.

Dan making new friends at a small village near Queen Elizabeth National Park, Uganda, 2012

Three projects stood out to us that were creative and had the potential to change the lives of the people involved.

The Tailors of Masindi

We traveled to Masindi to visit Dan's friend Kendall, who was going to travel with us for a few days. Kendall was excited to show us around her community. We met two adorable little girls who lived in the house next door to her and then walked around the Masindi market, amazed at the variety of products for sale in the open-air setting. It looked like a Walmart without the building. Fresh produce, meat, shoes, clothing of all types, hardware, auto parts—it all was there, piled on tables, hanging from racks, or simply arranged on the ground. It seemed like every time we turned a corner, another person would come up, greet Kendall, and give her a hug.

Kendall introduced us to a young man named Mustafa. He was a sort of jack-of-all-trades who helped the Americans in Masindi with a variety of things. He became our tour guide as we walked around and later our "boda boda" driver.

I should share a bit about transportation in Uganda. Getting around is a little more complicated than in the United States. People walk along the sides of the roads in large numbers. If you are traveling between towns, you may crowd onto a bus or into a van or small car with ten times more occupants than would reasonably fit in the vehicle. You probably will also share the ride with several babies, some chickens, and a goat. Shorter distances are traveled by boda boda, which is a small motorcycle. In every

Purchasing beautiful handmade quilts from David,
one of the tailors of Masindi, Uganda, 2012

town there are large numbers of young men on motorcycles waiting at the roadsides for passengers. It is not uncommon to see a
boda boda with a driver and two or three passengers behind him.
You might see a driver, a passenger, and then cargo, like lumber,
bricks, or a large stack of bananas or charcoal. Except in Kam-
pala, the country's capital, we never saw a helmet being worn.
Although we were reluctant to ride without helmets, there really
was no other option, so a few times, Rachel and I climbed aboard
together behind Mustafa, and off we went. "Slow, Mustafa. Drive
really slow!" we would tell him. The price of a boda boda ride was
usually less than twenty-five cents.

Kendall's project was very well conceived. She had met and
organized a group of seven tailors in Masindi whose primary

work was making colorful school uniforms for the thousands of school-age kids in the area. The tailors had lots of different colorful cloth scraps left over after making uniforms, shirts, skirts, dresses, and other items. Kendall's project involved organizing their efforts to use the leftover cloth to make beautiful quilts. We visited the street-side, single-room shops of several tailors and were impressed by the quality and beauty of the finished quilts. The work of one of the tailors, a man named David, really stood out to Rachel and me. We picked two of his quilts to buy and bring home. The price was somewhere around $50 per quilt. As I took out my wallet to pay David, Kendall quickly ushered us to the rear of the small shop. "You don't want to flash that amount of money around here," she told us. "That is more money than many people make in many months, and David could be in danger if it's known that he is carrying so much cash!" David was very happy to make a good sale that day.

The second part of the project involved finding a market for the quilts and teaching the tailors how to do the marketing themselves. As with all of the Peace Corps projects, the goal was to help the individuals develop skills needed to allow the project to go on after the volunteer had departed. As we traveled around during the next days, Kendall showed sample quilts to the owners and managers of resorts and high-end tourist shops that we visited, hoping to convince them to sell the beautiful, locally made quilts to their clientele.

Our colorful quilt is one of our favorite items that we brought back from Africa.

How to Keep the Elephants Out of the Garden

On the way to Queen Elizabeth National Park for our second safari of the trip, our driver Jimmy suggested that we stop at a nice resort to grab something cold to drink. As we walked up to the outdoor restaurant, Dan said, "Hey, there's Hailey!" Hailey, another Peace Corps volunteer, had been at her site near Queen Elizabeth for around a year longer than Dan had been in country. She also had one of the most interesting blogs on the Peace Corps' site, and I had been reading her posts almost daily for over a year. I felt like I knew her, having read about her Peace Corps experience from before she left home in the United States to the present. She seemed amazed that people like me were enjoying her daily ramblings about the ups and downs of her life in Uganda.

As we chatted, Hailey mentioned that she was waiting to meet a friend for lunch. A few minutes later, a young woman walked up the drive to the restaurant. We were a little embarrassed when we recognized her as someone we had passed on the road to the resort since we had not stopped to give her a ride. At home we would not think of picking up a hitchhiker, but in Africa, passing a single young American woman on the road seemed rude at best! Angela was working with local artists to create, produce, and sell a board game that taught environmental lessons to players. She brought out a game to show us. Jimmy asked how much the game would cost, and when Angela told him, he just smiled and said that it was very expensive by Ugandan standards.

The project that Hailey had organized around Queen Elizabeth was impressive and fun to hear about. This was especially the case since Hailey did not have a background in agriculture or biological sciences. One of the problems that she had identified when completing the needs assessment for her community was that the elephants that lived in the national park would come to the village's fields and gardens at night and trample and eat the crops. We would later see large numbers of elephants during a game drive in Queen Elizabeth National Park. The villagers had tried a variety of fencing and other strategies without success. The incursions had probably been going on for generations.

After doing some basic research, Hailey learned that elephants were afraid of another, much smaller creature found in Africa: the honey bee. She sought out and found a few beekeepers from a village not far away. They agreed to come and teach some farmers in Hailey's village about beekeeping. Together they designed a fence made up of beehives, strategically placed around the periphery of areas planted with crops. For the farmers, there was a double bonus. The presence of the bees kept the elephants away from the crops, increasing yield, and the honey produced by the bees was also a very good cash product that had not been part of the local economy before.

In bed that night, Rachel and I laughed, trying to imagine Hailey's mom and dad describing her work in Africa. Hailey looked like a young elementary school teacher or a Starbuck's barista. "Our daughter is training elephants in Uganda!"

Observing elephants in the wild was very different than our US experiences seeing them in a zoo. The photo on the cover of this book was taken during our safari in Queen Elizabeth National Park. In a boat moored fifty feet from shore, we watched a large group of elephants coming down to the water's edge to drink. It was very dry in the surrounding forest. We saw fifty or more elephants that afternoon. The scrum captured in the photo happened when a lone, young male attempted to join the herd drinking at the water's edge. He was much darker in color than the others. Three males joined together and charged him, pushing him away from the herd. A minute later he regrouped and made a second attempt. Feet were stomping. Ears were flapping. Tusks were thrashing. Dust was flying. The three lighter colored elephants prevailed and the lone male retreated. He had not been injured that we could tell, but he had put on a dramatic display. Dan was able to capture the tussle on video with his camera.

Bringing Educational Technology to the Ishaka School of Nursing

After a frustrating first year living in a small village with little support from the local health department, Dan was able to change sites to a nursing school in a larger town, Ishaka. The Ishaka School of Nursing trained nursing students from all around the region, impacting health care for thousands of Ugandan residents. Dan's living situation improved significantly when he moved. The nursing school provided a house for him on the campus, and the town was much larger than his previous

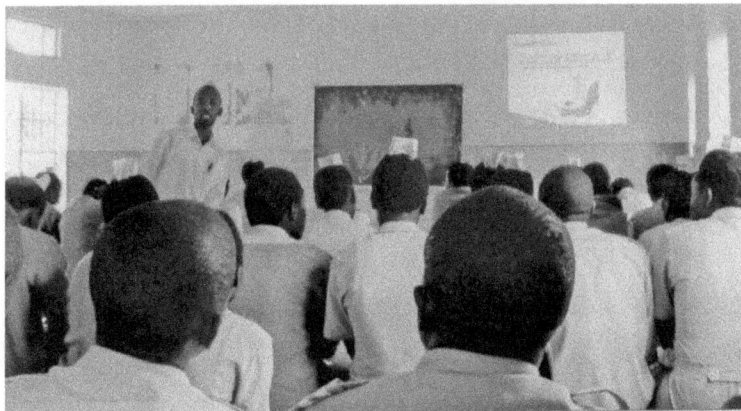

Nursing class using donated computer and projector,
Ishaka School of Nursing, Ishaka, Uganda, 2012

village. He had access to much better food and fresh produce, and he even had electricity and running water! As a registered nurse, Dan was excited for the opportunity to develop a project that would be a better match to his nursing experiences.

Dan's assessment of the nursing school's needs focused on teaching methods and the lack of technology in the nursing classes. The instructor would stand at the podium at the front of the classroom with the only textbook and read from the textbook while the students sat at their desks and took notes. It was like taking a college class on the telephone with no visual informa-tion to supplement the content.

In past conversations, Dan had made it clear to us that it was not a good idea to make donations or simply give things to people and organizations in Africa. The history of that kind of aid had created a culture of expectation and dependence. Dan explained that rather than donating malaria nets, for example, it would be better to help local people learn to produce the nets themselves. But in this case, Dan asked Rachel and me for some help getting his project started. His time was limited to his second year, and it was important to get things going.

Rachel and I were excited to give the first Imhoff/Dietz grant to the Ishaka School of Nursing to purchase two laptop computers and two projectors that would be used for PowerPoint presentations in nursing classes. Dan obtained the equipment and established a set of rules for its use and security. For example, the computers were for teaching classes, not for Facebook or porn! Over the course of a few months, Dan designed PowerPoint presentations for each nursing class lecture. These included photos, illustrations, and videos. He worked with instructors to help them become comfortable with the equipment and learn how best to use it in their classes. Dan taught some of them how to design their own PowerPoint presentations. Some were enthusiastic, and some were hesitant, but all instructors participated in the project. Dan said that the students encouraged their teachers to use the equipment in their classes.

Rachel and I were grateful for the opportunity to contribute to such an important project. The impact on the quality of education and training for nurses in the region could be significant, and the health care needs there are great. Our hope is that the use of this type of technology will be valued and will grow.

8

Never Pee on a Large Crocodile

Rachel and I had several exciting wild animal encounters during our Africa trip. The closest call that we experienced happened during a boat trip on the Nile River. We had traveled from Masindi to Murchison Falls National Park, a two-hour drive on dirt roads, along with Kendall, Dan's fellow Peace Corps volunteer, who was joining us for a few days of travel. We checked in at the Red Chili Camp, our lodging for the night. As we were eating lunch at the open-air café at Red Chili, a young woman approached our picnic table and asked if she could join us. Her name was Allison, and she had just completed her two-year Peace Corps assignment in Madagascar. She was traveling the length of Africa before heading home to California. I was amazed at her independence, a young American woman traveling by herself through Africa. She had traveled to the Red Chili Camp from Masindi on the back of a boda boda! We invited her to join us and sort of adopted her for the next few days.

After lunch we arranged a boat trip on the Nile to see animals and to view the foot of Murchison Falls from the water. The boat was long and slender, with two seats on each side of the boat and a narrow aisle running between them. The boat seated fourteen people plus the captain, who manned the motor at the rear of the boat. Another group from Germany was on board with us, but the boat was not full.

During the first part of the trip, we saw lots of hippos, crocodiles, and baboons. We were a bit nervous when we approached a mother hippo and baby and the mother disappeared under the water. The music from *Jaws* was playing in my head! We made our way to Murchison Falls and motored around the base of the falls. Though smaller than Niagara Falls in North America, Murchison was still impressive. We had walked around the top of the falls that morning, before arriving at our lodging for the night.

Once our boat ride was again under way, Kendall told our captain that she needed to pee. He smiled and said that he knew a place where he could land the nose of the boat on shore, and she could step off and take care of her business. It took about ten minutes to reach the site. The captain ran the nose of the boat onto the shore, where tall grass grew down to the river's edge. He looked at Kendall and said, "Safe place." Kendall began to make her way to the front of the boat, and Allison announced that she would go with her. Even in the wilds of Africa, women always want to have company using the restroom!

As Kendall was about to step out of the boat, one of the German passengers yelled, "No! Stop! Crocodile!" Hidden in the tall grass was a very large crocodile. I estimated its length at ten to twelve feet. It was thick in the belly and had a long snout and lots of visible teeth. The crocodile responded to the commotion by launching itself toward the water. From where I sat on the closest side of our narrow boat, it looked like it was coming right at the boat. More specifically, it looked like it was coming right at me. It landed in the water right next to the boat, and I felt the spray from its big splash. Everyone in the boat looked frozen, and no one said a word, until our captain announced, "Now it is safe!"

Kendall and Allison decided that they would pass up the opportunity to step out of the boat. Being an experienced traveler in Africa, Kendall walked to the back of the boat, squatted near the edge, lifted her skirt, and peed into the water. As we were backing away from the shore, a group of baboons ran out of the jungle and made threatening vocalizations at us. Like the crocodile, they did not seem to want to share their territory with a boatload of visitors.

That evening, as we played an African card game with Jimmy, our driver, we decided that we would trust our instincts when it came to risky situations, even if our "guides" assured us everything was safe. Each card in the game described the characteristics of an African animal. The animal with the greatest weight won the hand. I'm sure that we were all thinking that the crocodile that had almost landed in our boat was the ultimate winner that day.

Crossing the equator, rural Uganda, 2012.
We thought the sign would be bigger!

9

The Boys and the French Dictionary

Rachel and I were somewhat anxious about crossing the border from Uganda into Rwanda. A driver from our previous night's lodging at Lake Bunyoni dropped us off on the Uganda side of the border, and we crossed into Rwanda late in the morning. On the ride we had passed a United Nations refugee camp for people fleeing from the Democratic Republic of Congo. That was not the last time I experienced a strange feeling as I thought about how close we were to potential danger from insurgents in the DRC. We went through a very rustic set of customs buildings at the border, two stops on the Uganda side and two stops on the Rwanda side. We were glad to see our driver from the Kinigi Guest House, our lodging for the next few nights, pull up after a wait of about an hour. The driver did not speak English, and he drove very fast, even though the roads were dirt and lined with pedestrians and school kids walking home from school.

After arriving in Kinigi, and settling in at the guest house, Rachel and I decided to walk to the staging area for the mountain gorilla trek that we would do the following morning. It was a fifteen-minute walk from the guest house. On the way back, we passed a school that was letting out for the afternoon. The kids coming out looked to be high school–age. Five teenage boys approached us and said hello.

"Hi. I'm Peter," said one of the boys. "These are my schoolmates. Where are you from?"

We told him we were from St. Louis in the United States.

All of the boys smiled and nodded. "Oh, St. Louis. Yes," said Peter. "Could we walk with you and practice our English?"

Rachel and I both smiled and nodded. "That would be fine," I said.

For the next few minutes we walked together as they asked Rachel and me questions about our lives in the United States and told us a little about their school and school life. There were lots of smiles and laughter, and we were having a nice time with our new friends.

"Do you have children?" Peter asked us.

"Yes, we have three children," Rachel said. "They are older than you and out of school now."

"I bet they were very good students," Peter said.

"Actually, they all were very good students," I said.

"We are all very good students too," Peter said. "We work very hard!"

All of Peter's mates nodded.

Peter noticed my camera and asked if he could take our picture. The voice in my head told me that I didn't know these boys, and handing them our only camera might not be the best idea, so I declined. Without skipping a beat, Peter asked, "Then could you take our picture and send me a copy? I can give you my e-mail address."

The Internet is everywhere, I thought. "Sure, I'll take your picture, boys!"

Peter and his four friends posed and I took their picture. It turned out pretty good. Peter ripped a piece of paper out of a

Peter and his mates: the real boys searching for a French dictionary, Kinigi, Rwanda, 2012

notebook and wrote down his e-mail address. During the sponta-
neous photo shoot, other boys noticed what was happening and
joined our entourage. Soon there were ten boys walking with us!

Before long, we arrived at the driveway of the Kinigi Guest
House. As we started to turn in, Peter stopped us. "I have something very important to ask you," Peter said. The other boys
looked at us expectantly.

Here it comes, I thought.

"We have all been studying very hard for our French exami-
nations that are next week," Peter said. "But we have a problem."

All of the boys nodded.

"We do not have a dictionary! Without a dictionary we will
not be able to pass," Peter said with great sincerity.

All of the boys suddenly looked very sad and looked down
at the ground.

"But if you could give us just ten thousand francs, then we
could purchase a dictionary, and then we would be able to pass
our French exams!"

All of the boys looked up, more hopeful and happy.

"If you help us buy the dictionary, we promise to share it!"

All of the boys nodded.

"If you could give us twenty thousand francs, then we could
buy an even better French dictionary, and we promise we would
share that too!" Peter beamed. "Then we could do even better on
our exams!" The other boys beamed too.

I looked at Rachel, and we both smiled. What a great pitch!

It was creative. It was sincere. Who could deny the value of a nice dictionary? Sadly, that little voice in my head told me that our ten or twenty thousand francs would be spent at the local grocery and liquor store long before a dictionary could be purchased.

We politely declined the request but assured Peter that we would e-mail him the picture. He just smiled and laughed. Peter's facial expression seemed to say, *Hey, it was worth a shot!* We shook hands and turned in to the driveway to the guest house. Peter and the boys continued down the road.

Rachel and I decided that Peter had a great future ahead of him in a profession like automobile sales or telemarketing.

10

Gorillas in the Mist: Gorilla Trekking in the Mountains of Rwanda

One of my favorite movies is *Gorillas in the Mist* starring Sigourney Weaver. The movie depicts the life of Dian Fossey and her work trying to protect the mountain gorillas in what is now Rwanda. At the time of our Africa trip, there were fewer than nine hundred mountain gorillas left in the wild, anywhere in the world. These special survivors live in the Virunga Mountains in an area shared by Uganda, Rwanda, and the Democratic Republic of Congo.

As we planned our Africa trip, one of the most anticipated experiences was trekking in the Virunga Mountains in Rwanda to see mountain gorillas in their natural habitat. Rachel and I arranged for trekking permits for ourselves and my son Dan with a government office in Rwanda several months before our trip. The permits cost $500 per person and assigned us a specific date for our trek. We were told that we would be in a group of eight to ten people and that there was only one trek per day to see a given family group of gorillas. The trek might take a few hours or several hours, depending on where the particular group had spent the night. Once we found the group, we would have an hour or so to hang out with them and take pictures. There would be no fences, moats, or barriers between us and our closest primate relatives. The terrain was described as difficult, but we felt ready for the challenge.

The morning of the trek, Rachel, Dan, and I were up at six o'clock for coffee and a simple breakfast. We arrived at the staging area about seven and checked in. We would be assigned to our group once everyone else arrived. A colorful group of African dancers in traditional garb was performing for the trekkers. We had a moment of panic when Rachel announced that she could not find her wallet. We searched through her knapsack without success and then returned to the office where we had checked in. There was Rachel's wallet, sitting on the counter where she had set it down. We felt blessed that it had not disappeared.

There were approximately eighty trekkers heading out for the day. We were divided into ten groups, each of which was assigned to a different family group of gorillas. Rachel and I were assigned to the Ugenda group. This family group included two silverback males, two babies, and a total of twelve gorillas. Our group of trekkers was made up of eight people: Rachel and me, Dan, two middle-aged couples from Germany, and a young man from California. Dan, Rachel, and I piled into a Toyota pickup truck for a one-hour drive to the trailhead. The road was more of a rocky trail, and we averaged about five miles per hour as we bounced up and down over the rocks. We likely would have gone faster walking! My butt was sore, as was the top of my head, by the time we arrived at the trailhead.

At the trailhead we met our guides, John and Emmanuel. Each of us was handed a tall walking stick and offered the services of a porter to carry our packs and provide any assistance that we might need. Even though our group looked like it included a wide variety of fitness levels, everyone declined the assistance of a porter. John chose two of the porters to join us anyway, which turned out to be a very good thing. John reported that he expected the hike to the Ugenda group to take a little more than two hours. He was in radio contact with spotters in the jungle. We headed out, with the first part of the trail meandering through small villages and cultivated farm fields. As we passed each home or farm, small children would run out, waving and calling, "Hullo! Hullo!" We waved and returned the greetings.

When we reached the edge of the jungle, John informed us that the trek was now going to become more difficult and steep. We were entering the actual mountains, and since gorillas don't follow trails, we wouldn't be following any either. We would be bushwhacking through the jungle and climbing in elevation. John and Emmanuel had large machetes to chop away the vegetation. Without an introduction, another man joined us, armed with a military-style automatic weapon. John said that he would be accompanying us to protect us from elephants or other large animals we might encounter. We wondered if he was also protecting us from two-legged creatures that might cross over the Congo border.

We followed our guides through the jungle and up the side of the mountain. It was the most difficult hiking that Rachel and I had ever done, and more than once, a porter grabbed the back of my waist as I slipped on a wet rock or tripped on a root. One porter took responsibility for one of the German women and sort of dragged her up the mountain. After about an hour, John turned toward us and told us that we now were entering an area of stinging nettles. To our surprise, John and the other guides and porters reached into their packs and put on a second pair of pants over their current pants and a second long-sleeved shirt. Rachel and I had read about recommended clothing and had worn long-sleeved shirts and long pants, but they were relatively thin. We had brought leather gloves, though, which we put on. The German couples were much less prepared, and the guys had short-sleeved shirts. No one else had gloves. The leather gloves were a godsend for pushing nettles away, but we were repeatedly stung through our hiking pants.

A little while later, John stopped us and had us gather around him. We were getting close now, he said, and we should be very quiet and respectful of the gorillas' habitat. He reminded us to try to stay at least seven meters from the gorillas and if approached, to kneel and look down at the ground, trying to appear docile. I didn't think feeling docile would be a problem. We walked just a few more minutes and saw a large silverback male sitting against a tree. He looked huge. We all got out our cameras and started taking pictures. As we quietly explored the area, we found first one and then a second baby gorilla and then a female who looked like a new mother. She was slowly eating bamboo, and she watched us as we watched her. It took some doing, but finally I was able to take a picture of Dan with a gorilla in the picture just behind him.

One of the most moving parts of the experience for me was that many of the gorillas made eye contact with me as I was looking at them. We were the weird creatures entering their domain for a few minutes every day. What were they thinking as they watched us stumbling around with our brand-new REI clothing and fancy cameras?

The most exciting moment of the day occurred when I was busy snapping pictures, and one of the other trekkers warned us that the other silverback male was coming down the side of the mountain toward Rachel and me. Our guides had warned us to stay seven meters away from the gorillas, but that didn't mean that the gorillas followed the same protocol. As the large male approached, I made eye contact with John, our guide, my nervous look asking what I was supposed to do.

John smiled at me and said, "Just stand still. He looks like he's pretty relaxed." The silverback walked slowly down the hill, passing Rachel and me. He was so close that we could have reached out and touched him.

We stayed for a little over an hour, and then John let us know it was time to head back. Each gorilla group was visited just once per day for an hour. The physical environment was not what I had expected. I had pictured a family of gorillas eating and playing in a more open forest environment. A jungle environment on the side of an inactive volcano is much different and more difficult to navigate. Just finding a good spot to stand to take a picture was often challenging.

The trip down the mountain was quicker than the trip up, but the going was still sometimes treacherous. I again was glad that the porters were there to offer a hand when needed. Dan, Rachel, and I were tired but happy to have had such a rare encounter with an endangered species. Once back down, we were given certificates documenting our adventure, and Rachel and I bought a cheesy T-shirt celebrating our trek to see the Ugenda group. Back at the guest house, we sipped a beer and looked at the most amazing pictures any of us had ever taken.

Dian Fossey is buried near the site of her research station in the mountains that we visited. Her work continues, as scientists and rangers learn from and do their best to protect the remaining mountain gorillas.

*Endangered mountain gorillas from the Ugenda Family,
Virunga Mountains, Rwanda, 2012*

PART 3
US Adventures

11

A Surprise at the Chase Park Plaza

Some travel adventures take place close to home. One of those adventures turned out to be an important one for both Rachel and me. I met Rachel less than four weeks before my fiftieth birthday. Dating at forty-nine had sometimes seemed awkward, and Rachel was five years younger than me. I had some anxiety about moving into the next decade.

We had probably gone on five or six dates in the four weeks leading up to my birthday, which I thought had gone pretty well, when Rachel invited me to her Central West End apartment for a special birthday dinner. Rachel's stepdaughter, Christina, was staying with her for a few weeks before moving to Europe but would probably be out for most of the evening. "Why don't you come over around six thirty?" Rachel suggested a few days before as we talked on the phone. "And Tim, if you'd like to bring your toothbrush and a change of clothes, I think that would be okay too."

"That sounds like a very cool birthday celebration," I said, excited about the sleepover invite.

On Saturday I packed up a small toiletry kit and a few extra clothes for the next day. I was still a little nervous about my birthday and the evening. I got dressed in my favorite black jeans and a black turtleneck. I liked that look for whatever reason. I arrived at Rachel's apartment right on time, which was my habit. She greeted me with a nice birthday hug and kiss, and we walked up the stairs to her apartment. Rachel was wearing black dress slacks, a red silky blouse, and heels. Her shoulder-length blonde hair and subtle makeup were beautiful. Christina was just getting ready to leave. Rachel said that Christina had a "Match date" that evening. We laughed because we had met through Match.com just a few weeks earlier.

"Well, did you bring your toothbrush, Tim?" Rachel asked.

"Yep. I have an overnight bag in the car," I said.

"Why don't you go get it?" Rachel suggested, giving me a big smile.

This is going to be a great birthday! I thought. I ran down to the car, and when I got back upstairs to her apartment, Rachel took the bag and set it in the entryway.

"We can put it away a bit later," she said. "I thought maybe we could go for a walk around the Central West End before we eat. Maybe we can even find a cool place for a glass of wine."

I was like putty in her hands. She could have suggested that we run around the block naked, and I probably would have agreed! We said goodbye to Christina, who gave Rachel a hug.

"Have a fun night, Mom," I heard Christina say to Rachel. That made me smile.

Rachel lived on Lindell Boulevard, just a block down from the St. Louis Cathedral. It's a great neighborhood for walking and exploring interesting shops and restaurants. We held hands and walked around the different streets for about an hour. It was nice holding hands and talking as we window-shopped. Eventually, we ended up at the entrance to the Chase Park Plaza, a landmark hotel in St. Louis. The Chase is several stories tall and has a classy vibe. I had been there only to see movies. The Chase has a classic older theater on the main floor that sometimes shows independent films that aren't playing in the major theaters.

We went inside the Chase and walked through much of the main lobby and first floor. We passed at least three bars and restaurants. Rachel seemed to have an idea of what she was looking for. "I think there are cooler bars here than these," Rachel told me.

"Wherever you'd like to stop would be fine," I said.

We walked to a bank of elevators, and Rachel pushed the "up" button. "I know one other spot that I think is on the sixth floor."

We went up to the sixth floor and got off. The hallway was deserted and looked like most any hotel hallway. I didn't see any signs announcing a cocktail lounge or other public area. Rachel guided us down the hall to one of the last doors and pulled out a plastic room key and quickly swiped it through the lock. "This is the place I was thinking, Tim."

As we walked into the suite, I felt like all of my senses were being bombarded at once. Rachel was still holding my hand.

Every surface in the hotel room seemed to be covered with flickering candles. There must have been a hundred of them. Soft jazz music was playing on the Bose stereo system in the living room. A delicious aroma was coming from a small kitchen area off to the side. "Happy birthday, Tim! I thought your fiftieth birthday should be very special!" Rachel said and gave me a kiss. I don't think I have ever been more surprised. I stood looking around the suite. *How did she arrange this?* I wondered.

We walked through the suite. It had a living room area, a small kitchen, a separate bedroom, and a large bath with a Jacuzzi tub and a separate walk-in shower. Candles were lit and sparkling in every room. My overnight bag was already in the bedroom, as was Rachel's travel bag.

"Christina was my coconspirator," Rachel said. "While we were walking, she brought our bags and all of the preparations and set up the room. She did a great job."

"She sure did!" I said.

Rachel went to the kitchen and poured two glasses of champagne. The bottle had already been opened and was chilling in an ice bucket. "This is Domaine Carneros from Napa in California," Rachel said. "Christina and I visited there last year, and I bought a case. It is really delicious."

Who is this woman? I thought. *I don't know anyone who has ever visited Napa, and I don't know anyone who buys nice champagne by the case!*

We sat in the living room and sipped our champagne while soft jazz played in the background. Rachel told me about some of her travel experiences. She was an experienced traveler and had even lived in foreign countries when she worked as an IT consultant. She had also lived all over the United States. We had that in common, which was unusual for St. Louis residents.

A little while later, Rachel announced that dinner was probably done, and she took a dish out of the oven. Rachel said that she and Christina had made paella, a Spanish dish with rice, chicken, veggies, and a variety of spices. She took two large wine glasses from the counter and a bottle of red wine.

"Champagne was for before dinner," she said. "A nice Silver Oak cabernet is our pairing with dinner. I think you'll like it."

"Those are really big glasses, Rachel," I observed.

"Champagne goes in skinny flute glasses. White wine goes in medium-sized regular glasses. Cabernet tastes best in a large glass like this," Rachel said. "It allows the cabernet to open up. You'll see the wine actually gets better, the longer it sits in the glass. These are Riedel glasses. They are really nice. Christina brought them from home."

The wine tasted very smooth and was better than any of the red wines that I had tried before. I reminded myself that I was no connoisseur and had mostly purchased wines at a very different price point. I remembered the wine tasting party that I had hosted for work friends several years earlier. Everyone was asked to bring an "interesting" wine to the party to share. Everyone brought a bottle of the same brand of cheap wine. It came in a number of varietals and sold for around four dollars for a really large bottle. We were a classy group!

The paella was delicious. I had tasted paella once or twice, but it had been many years. I was impressed that Rachel had made something from scratch and not just purchased a premade appetizer or dinner.

After champagne, dinner, and a glass or two of cabernet, my head was sort of spinning, and we both felt warm and relaxed. Rachel and I sat together on the sofa, listening to the music and watching the candles burn. We talked about a million things, getting to know each other better.

Eventually, we got ready for bed and crawled under the crisp sheets and soft comforter of our king-size bed. "Thanks for the most amazing birthday I've ever had, Rachel. You know how to make an impression, that's for sure. No one I tell about tonight is going to believe it!"

"That was my goal, Tim. I hope you'll always remember tonight with a big smile on your face."

We spent the rest of the evening making sure that it would be a really big smile.

We woke up the next morning a little later than usual for both of us. As we looked around our suite, the first thing we noticed was the state of the candles. "Oops, I think we may be in trouble," Rachel said with a laugh. All of the hundred or so candles were out. That was the good news. The bad news was that they had melted all over whatever furniture they had been placed on. Pools of hard candle wax could be found on every surface. And the furniture looked very expensive.

Rachel and I did our best to gently scrape off all of the melted wax from the coffee table, side tables, book shelves, dresser, credenza, kitchen counter, sink, bathtub, window sills, and any other places we found it. Most of the wax came off pretty well, but it looked like the dark wooden furniture would never be quite the same. *At least the room is in her name, I thought.*

We cleaned up the dishes and packed up everything that Christina had brought.

"I think we need to at least try out the Jacuzzi tub," I suggested. "We have plenty of time." So we enjoyed a leisurely soak in the Jacuzzi. Rachel had even brought bubble bath. *Jeez, this woman is really detail-oriented!* I thought.

After our soak, we left the room keys on the table, gathered our bags, and walked back to Rachel's apartment, picking up Starbucks on the way.

Christina was in the kitchen when we arrived. She had the biggest smile on her face! "So how was it, guys?" Christina asked.

"It was the most amazing birthday anyone has ever had!" I answered. And it was!

12

Homeless in Muscatine

Not all travel adventures are exotic and filled with colorful sights and characters. Some are quite simple but make you happy when you can say that you made it there and back again. I had that kind of an adventure on a very cold winter day in Rachel's hometown, Muscatine, Iowa.

Rachel and I had been dating for a few months, and she had invited me to join her on a trip to Muscatine to visit her family and spend Christmas Eve with them. She had also arranged to get her hair cut while we were there. Even though Rachel had lived in St. Louis for several years, she continued to go back to Muscatine every few months to get her hair cut by the stylist she had gone to for many years. A five-hour drive for a haircut seemed a bit long to me, but it gave her an excuse to see her family more often than she might have otherwise.

Muscatine is a small river town on the Mississippi River in eastern Iowa. It is a farming region, and major employers include factories that make furniture and tires. Historically, it also was a leading manufacturer of buttons made out of shells. Buttons have to be made somewhere! The University of Iowa in Iowa City is about twenty-five miles away. Rachel's dad, Gil Dietz, was the editor of the Muscatine daily newspaper for many of his working years, and he and Rachel's Mom, Virginia, continue to be active in the community.

Rachel and I made the five-hour drive north from St. Louis to Muscatine on a Friday afternoon, the day before Christmas Eve. The roads were dry, but the weather was cold, and the temperature continued to drop during the drive. When we arrived in the early evening, the temperature was ten degrees. There was quite a bit of snow on the ground and piled up on the sides of the roads and parking lots. We filled up the gas tank, checked into our motel, and then made our way to Rachel's mom and dad's condo.

Rachel's brother Pat and his family came over to share a Dietz family dinner. I had met them just once before. Pat and his wife Lori had three kids, Miles, Paige, and Madison. Miles was in high school, Paige was in middle school, and Madison was in elementary school. Dating and meeting my girlfriend's family was a little weird at the age of fifty, but Rachel's family was open and welcoming.

When Rachel and I woke up Saturday morning, the temperature had dipped to six degrees, and it was a little windy. St. Louis rarely got that cold. But I had grown up and gone to college in

Madison, Wisconsin, and remembered days when the temperature stayed below zero all day. One did not spend a lot of time outside on those days. Weather forecasters would warn listeners, "Human flesh will freeze within thirty seconds of exposure!" If your car was parked outside, you felt lucky if it started. I was glad that Rachel and I had filled the tank with gas when we arrived the night before. Our car started up just fine.

Rachel's hair appointment was at 9:15 a.m. Our plan was for her to drop me off at the public library in downtown Muscatine and come back for me in two or three hours. A few hours of browsing the shelves and reading sounded relaxing. At about five after nine, we pulled up in front of the public library. I put on my gloves, gave Rachel a kiss, stepped out of her BMW, and waved as she drove away. I zipped my coat up to try to protect my neck from the wind and walked to the main entrance. I pulled on the door handle. It didn't open. I pushed on the door handle. It still didn't open. I looked through the glass doors. A few lights were on, but most were not. I looked at the stenciled sign on the door. It said that Saturday hours were 9:00 a.m. to 5:00 p.m. Above the stenciled sign was a message typed on white paper: "Closed on Christmas Eve."

I paused and then laughed to myself. *Duh. It is Christmas Eve! What were we thinking?* I stood for a minute or two, just staring inside the library. It looked warm and inviting. I reached in my coat pocket for my cell phone. It wasn't there. I never put it in my pants pocket, but I checked anyway. It wasn't there either. I knew that I'd had it when I left the motel. In my mind I retraced our drive over from the motel and could picture my cell phone, sitting in the cup holder of Rachel's car. It was still there.

I thought, *Okay, I'm in downtown Muscatine. It's six degrees outside. I don't have a phone. I don't know the town very well at all. I don't know where Rachel's family lives or where the stylist is located. The library is closed. I could freeze in minutes. Why did Rachel take me here? Why did Rachel leave me here? Why did she need to drive five hours to get a stupid haircut? Why did we forget that it was Christmas Eve and everything was bound to be closed?*

At least I was in the main downtown area of Muscatine. I just needed to find an alternate location to warm up and hang out for a few hours. I began to walk down one of the main streets. I passed a few restaurants and bars, but all were closed. I passed several shops and offices. They were all closed as well. Looking around, I noticed that there were no people on the sidewalks. There were no cars traveling on the streets. This really was a sleepy river town, especially early on the morning of Christmas Eve.

After about an hour, I was still walking up and down the main streets of downtown Muscatine. I had not encountered any place that was open, and I was getting very cold, especially my fingers, toes, and ears. At last I came around a corner and found an open store, Stiles Family Hardware. I laughed, both with relief and because Rachel had mentioned that in high school she had worked at Stiles. The store was a few blocks from the library, so I decided to just hang out for a while and then make my way back to the library to meet Rachel in an hour or so. The store was pretty small. It didn't take long to walk all of the aisles. I didn't need any paint, mousetraps, nails, lightbulbs, or grass seed. I felt sort of like a homeless person, just trying to find a warm place to get out of the cold. I hoped that I did not have one of those "snot icicles" when I came in from the cold! I imagined that I looked sort of like a homeless person to the woman behind the counter too, who began to look at me a bit suspiciously as I walked the aisles. She probably knows everyone who shops at Stiles, I thought.

Looking back on it, I realize that I probably should have explained my predicament to the counter person. She would have thought it was funny and maybe would have offered me a cup of coffee. But at the time, I felt embarrassed and just avoided her eye contact. That probably made me look even more out of place. When I thought that she was ready to call someone for backup, I decided to head back to the library, hoping that Rachel's hair appointment would be done early rather than later than anticipated.

Rachel pulled up in front of the library a little after eleven. When I got in the car, she asked why I was waiting outside. "It's a long story," I told her. "Let's go find someplace warm, and I'll tell you about it."

13

It's Raining Hairy Bears!

In October 2006, Rachel and I took a trip to Cape Cod, staying at country inns and bed-and-breakfasts in a few scenic towns along the Cape. Our final destination was the Red Inn in Provincetown on the tip of Cape Cod. We were scheduled to arrive the day before Halloween. From our reading, we knew about Provincetown's history of being welcoming to the gay and lesbian community. We were looking forward to the location of the Red Inn right on the beach and to exploring the culture of P-Town.

We arrived at the Red Inn in the late afternoon. It was a sunny day, and families with kids were playing on the beach. As promised, the inn was right on the water. All rooms faced the ocean, with sliding glass doors and a small concrete porch area in front. Ten steps led directly down to the sand. The ocean was calm, with gentle waves lapping at the sand a few hundred feet from our door. The sunrise promised to be spectacular.

After getting settled in our room, we walked down to the office area of the inn and visited with Mark, one of the owners. He was a handsome man of about forty-five with a bushy brown mustache.

"We will be having a special Halloween dinner tomorrow night," Mark said. "All of our staff will be in costume, and I've heard some will be outrageous!"

Rachel and I looked at each other and nodded. "That sounds like fun!" Rachel said. "Sign us up. How about around seven?"

Mark made a note in his reservation book. "You're all set," he said. "By the way, have you guys heard about Hairy Bear Weekend?"

"No, I don't think we have," I said.

Mark laughed. "Well, as you walk around P-Town this weekend, I imagine that you'll figure it out."

Not wanting to look like unsophisticated travelers, Rachel and I just smiled and let his comment pass.

We decided to take a walk around town to get a feel for things and find a restaurant for dinner. Provincetown was a cute seaside community with tree-lined streets, interesting shops, and lots of restaurants and bars. After walking and window-shopping for an hour or so, I turned to Rachel. "Have you noticed anything about the people we have been passing on the sidewalks?"

Rachel laughed. "I wondered if you were going to say something before I did." Nearly all of the people we had encountered were good-sized male couples with beards. We looked at each other and said simultaneously, "Hairy bears."

It turned out that the weekend was a gathering for hairy bears, and most hotels and inns were booked up with gay couples of that type. Rachel and I would likely stand out in a crowd. How fun! We always enjoyed new experiences!

We found a cozy restaurant for dinner where a few other couples were dining too. All were hairy bears. The waitstaff were all guys and were quite gregarious. Because the crowd was small, the staff shared funny stories with the diners as a group. "Jason, tell the boys about the time the homeless guy was found sleeping in the storage room. Oh, tell Tim and Rachel too." It was a fun evening. We stayed for a few hours, said good-bye to our new friends, and walked back to the inn.

When we got back to the Red Inn, Mark was in the reception area. "Hi, guys! So did you run into any hairy bears?" he asked with a wink.

"Yeah, we did," I said.

"Actually, the restaurant was filled with them," Rachel added.

We shared a laugh and described our enjoyable dinner.

"I should let you know that the weather is supposed to turn during the night," Mark said. "I don't think it will be anything serious, but it might put a crimp in some of your outside plans for the weekend."

"Thanks for the heads-up. We're pretty good at just going with the flow," Rachel said. We said good night and retired to our room.

Rachel and I woke up the next morning to a very different view from our room. The entire beach was gone, and the Atlantic

Before and during a tropical storm,
Provincetown, Massachusetts, 2006

Ocean was now splashing against the cement foundation of the Inn. The wind was blowing a strong rain against the sliding glass doors, and the waves were pretty big. We were still in our adventurous travel mindset, so Rachel took a few pictures of me in front of the sliding glass doors with the ominous Atlantic Ocean behind me.

As I looked down, I realized that the waves were only a few feet below the cement porch of our room. "Um, Rachel, if the water rises much higher, we could be totally flooded out."

Rachel walked over to where I was standing by the sliding glass door. We looked out at the gray, angry ocean together. "We better keep our eyes open, sweetie," said Rachel. "Let's go ask Mark if we should be worried or whether we should move our stuff out."

We walked down to the dining area of the inn, and Mark was there pouring coffee for a few guests. When he came to our table, we asked him about the storm.

"Oh, you'll be fine, guys. I've owned the inn for fifteen years and lived in P-Town for twenty-five. The inn has never flooded," he assured us. A moment later, the power went out.

Mark called around and reported to the guests in the dining room that power was out over most of Provincetown. A little later, he let everyone know that the special Halloween dinner planned for that evening would probably be canceled. Because of the storm, the staff would have more pressing things to deal with, both at the inn and at their homes.

Rachel and I went back to our room and checked the status of the waves. They appeared to have moved a little closer to our room's cement porch. We decided to move our suitcases to the car, just in case. Since we were going to the car, we decided that we might as well take a drive around town to see if we could find an open store to stock up on supplies. "Let's pick up some food and water," I suggested.

"And wine!" Rachel added.

The wind and rain were strong, but the roads around Provincetown were passable. After a half hour or so, we started seeing lights on in some of the buildings. We found an open convenience store and purchased lots of junk food and beverages. There was not really anywhere else to go, so we made our way back to the Red Inn. Rachel and I hunkered down and spent the day watching the storm and the level of the waves. Mid-afternoon, the storm began to die down, and the water began to recede. The power came back on in the early evening.

The restaurant at the Red Inn did not open for the Halloween dinner. So we ventured out in the evening and found another restaurant that was open and enjoyed a quiet dinner. We weren't sure what had happened to the crowds of hairy bears. We assumed that most were hibernating back in their man caves.

14

The Omega Couple: All Alone in the Big Apple

Rachel and I made several trips to New York City in the few years that my son Dan lived in Manhattan. He had moved to New York for a summer nursing internship at the Sloan-Kettering Cancer Hospital and then worked there for two years after graduating from college at the University of Missouri. One of our financial advisors in St. Louis owned a condominium on West Sixty-Sixth Street in Manhattan, and he made the condo available to some of his clients, without charge. Rachel and I were fortunate to take advantage of this offer several times.

The condo was on the twenty-fifth floor of a high-rise building. The building had a doorman and a concierge desk in the lobby. Lincoln Center and Juilliard were right next door. We were proud that we never took a taxi in Manhattan and instead were always able to take the subway or trains to get to our destinations. We also did lots of walking.

I had visited Manhattan a few times before for professional meetings and conferences. I always had felt a little intimidated by the reputation of New York City, the crowds, and the overall hustle and bustle. It's a long way from the lifestyle of the sedate Midwest. But during our trips, Rachel and I were surprised by the friendliness of the people we encountered. When we would stop on the sidewalk to look at our map, it was common for a doorman to come out of his building or for someone to stop on the sidewalk to see if he or she could help us with directions.

Once while walking to Dan's apartment in Chinatown, we passed a disheveled old man sitting on the sidewalk, talking to himself. We hurried past him. A few minutes later, as we were waiting for Dan outside his apartment, the same old man approached us. He stopped and smiled at us.

"Sir, you have a very pretty daughter!"

I looked at Rachel. She was smiling at him.

"Yes, she is a looker, that's for sure," I said.

"Why don't you join me for breakfast?" the man said. "My friend owns a place just around the corner, and they have the best breakfast in the city!"

We thanked him and told him that we had breakfast plans already with our son and some of his friends.

One of our more interesting New York experiences happened in August 2011, when Hurricane Irene roared up the East Coast toward New York City. We had arrived in Manhattan a few days before and had gotten settled in the condo. We watched the news and weather carefully to hear the predictions for landfall and the potential impact on the city. We looked out the large windows of the condo onto the neighboring buildings and wondered how the building would fare with hurricane-force winds. We had scheduled a cocktail party with our daughter Laurel, her boyfriend Matt, and his parents Ed and Cindy. They all lived within driving distance of the city and were going to join us at the condo the next evening. We also had tickets to a Broadway play, *Million Dollar Quartet.*

As the storm approached, the city prepared for the worst. People in low-lying areas were told to evacuate. We were not concerned about flooding at our location, but it was becoming clear that Manhattan was going to be very different the day the hurricane was expected to hit. The city announced that the trains and subways would stop service the evening before the storm. The tens of thousands of people who worked in the hotels, restaurants, theaters, stores, and other businesses would need to leave Manhattan before the subways stopped running, leaving most of those businesses closed. We were told to prepare for the possibility of several days without power. Rachel and I had images of Hurricane Katrina in New Orleans running though our minds. We talked with our daughter Laurel and canceled the cocktail party.

We shopped at neighborhood food stores for food, water, and of course, wine. We looked through the condo but could not find flashlights, candles, or matches. Later we saw a notice from the building managers that candles were strictly prohibited because of the danger of fire in a high-rise building. We had to ask the doorman where we could find a hardware store, and he directed us to one a few blocks away. We purchased two of the last flashlights that the store had and lots of spare batteries. We talked a few times with John, the owner of the condo, who was back in St. Louis. He thought everything would be fine, but it might be a long day or two.

The morning of the hurricane was very quiet, especially for Manhattan. The sun was shining. The temperature was mild. There were very few pedestrians on the sidewalks and only a handful of yellow cabs cruising the streets. We went for a walk in Central Park and around the neighborhood. Most shops and businesses were closed up tight, but we did find a restaurant that was still open and stopped for breakfast. The employees must have lived close by and not needed to evacuate. The scene reminded me of an old Charlton Heston movie, *The Omega Man*. For the first part of the movie, his character appears to be the only survivor of a biological warfare disaster, living in Los Angeles. For Rachel and me, walking around deserted Manhattan streets felt like that. We were the Omega Couple!

In the afternoon we hunkered down in our twenty-fifth-floor condo. The wind picked up in the late afternoon, and the rain started. The weather reports made it sound like it would not be a direct hit, but there would be strong winds, lots of rain, and flooding in lower-lying areas. City leaders were especially worried about flooding in the subway system.

Rachel and I were lucky. We did not lose power that night at all. We watched the strong, sometimes horizontal rain bands hitting our windows and surrounding buildings. We looked for old ladies in rocking chairs and cows flying by but did not see anything Oz-like. We did enjoy snacking on all of the fresh food we had purchased and drinking some of the wine.

In the morning Manhattan was mostly back to normal. The sky was clear. Doormen were cleaning the sidewalks and entries to their buildings. Businesses were open. Subways were running. When we again walked to Central Park, several areas were taped off, warning of the danger of falling limbs from the trees. We walked to the Broadway theater where our tickets had gone unused the day before and were able to trade them in for another day.

The overall vibe of the city was something like "Hurricane? What's a little hurricane? We're New Yorkers!"

15

A Bucket List Race, or "It's Getting Mighty Caliente in Here!"

Rachel and I have enjoyed doing an occasional destination race when we travel. We have done 5Ks, 10Ks, and even a few half marathons. We had planned a trip to Sarasota, Florida, for a few days at the beginning of May 2013. When Rachel checked to see if there were any races during the days we were going to be there, she found just one. "Well, there is one 5K race that weekend, Tim. It's being sponsored by a resort north of Tampa. It's called the Bare Dare."

"Does that mean what I think it means?" I asked.

"Yep, a naked 5K."

We laughed as we read about the Bare Dare. It was described as a bucket list race and a national championship for nude racing. I don't know that running a 5K in the nude was on either of our bucket lists, but the more we talked, the more intrigued we became. A few days later, Rachel was surprised when I went ahead and signed us up for the race. I wasn't sure that we would follow through with it, but the fun we had just imagining the race was worth the registration fee.

As Rachel and I prepared for the trip, details around the Bare Dare were part of the planning. Who knew that choosing what clothes to bring would be so important in packing to visit a clothing-optional resort? The race was going to be at the Caliente Resort, north of Tampa. The website showed lots of young people, all beautiful and tan, lounging around the pool or in the cocktail lounge. It looked like a large property with a hotel, restaurants, two pools, and lots of homes and rentals. The race course ran through the streets of the property.

We laughed when Rachel read a blog post on the website for the race. "They just posted that they now have people from thirty states registered for the Bare Dare. The last two were from 'the Show-Me State.' Do you think that's us?" Rachel asked.

"I'm sure it is!" I said.

We traveled to Sarasota a few days before the Bare Dare. We relaxed at the Lido Beach Resort, walked on the beach, and visited a few of our favorite restaurants, including Pop's Sunset Grill in Nokomis and the Sandbar on Anna Maria Island. We frequently shared our predictions of what the race and the resort would be like and what made us most nervous. "What if everyone is young and beautiful, like in the pictures on the website?" Rachel asked.

"Then I think you will fit right in. I'm not sure about me."

"No, I mean it, Tim."

"Well, the articles on the website say that it's a mixed crowd and that people look like runners in any other 5K race," I said. "I don't think they'll be looking at us much anyway. What if we run into someone we know from work?" I asked with a smile. "That would be hysterical."

"Surprise! Hi, Doctor So-and-So!" Rachel said with a laugh.

Race day arrived, and the weather was perfect. It was sunny and in the upper seventies. I had printed out directions to the Caliente Resort, and we were on our way bright and early. It was a two-and-a-half-hour drive from Sarasota. We were both nervous but trying to hide it as best we could. As was our habit, I drove, and Rachel was the navigator. We found the correct exit off of the interstate but then got a little lost. Finally, I stopped at a convenience store to ask for help. It felt funny trying to figure out how to ask for directions: "Um, can you tell me how to get to the nudist resort?" Fortunately, as I was waiting in line, I looked at the directions again and saw that the turn we were looking for was seven miles down the road, not one mile. We just hadn't gone far enough.

We pulled into the drive to the Caliente Resort about forty-five minutes before race time. There was a guardhouse with a gate, and the resort looked pretty fancy. The attendant, who was dressed in regular street clothes, asked if we were there for the race and welcomed us. We drove in and followed the road around to a central parking area. We passed a few people walking and a few people in golf carts, all naked, except for shoes. It looked funny. We parked our car and looked at each other. "Well, here we are!" I said. "It's not too late to turn around."

Rachel smiled. "We came this far. I think we should just do it!"

We both laughed, nervously.

"Let's go find the registration area and see how everything works," Rachel said.

"Okay," I said. "Naked?"

"Yep. You know what they say. When in Rome."

We both stripped down to just our running shoes and matching Missouri Running Company hats. We left the rest of our clothes in the car. We sprayed on sunscreen, front and back. I laughed when I realized I did not have any pockets in which to put the keys to our rental car. I'd have to hold them, even during the race.

I took Rachel's hand, and off we went. We found the main clubhouse, and a sign pointed us to the registration tables. The young people manning the registration tables were dressed in khaki shorts and polo shirts, as were the Caliente staff. They gave Rachel and me wristbands, giving us access to the resort for the day. There were quite a few runners milling around, registering, warming up, or just standing around in small groups. All were naked, just like us.

As in most races, the runners were a mixture of ages. There were both men and women. There were lots of body types, and I was glad to see that not everyone looked like the young beautiful people on the website. As predicted, the runners looked like the kind of crowd you would see at any 5K race. Some of the women were very attractive, and I'm sure I wasn't the only guy glancing around but trying to not look too obvious. I was glad I had on sunglasses. I looked over at Rachel, and she was looking around at the scene, just like I was. I was struck by the realization that almost everyone was shaved or waxed smooth, both men and women.

Rachel and I signed in and spent a few minutes doing some warm-up jogging, testing out the feeling of running with all of our "stuff" bouncing up and down. We were surprised that it wasn't that bad, and after a few minutes, we got used to the motion and movement. Before we knew it, we were lining up for the start of the race. There were probably two hundred runners. Our plan was to go out slow and just enjoy the experience.

The race director welcomed the runners and gave us instructions about the course. The national anthem was played on a portable CD player, and then the race director sounded the horn, and we were off. Some people went out very fast. Others were slower than us, and there were a few walkers. The race course went through the streets of the resort. Some spectators sat in front of their houses or waved from their porches. All were nude. As we were running down a small cul-de-sac, I tripped on an irregularity in the road and had a close call. I caught myself before I fell and was no worse for wear. That would have been a painful landing with no clothing to protect skin and bones!

Rachel and I completed the race in about thirty minutes. We raised our arms as we crossed the finish line. Another couple finished just behind us. "Thanks, guys," the middle-aged man said. "We followed you the whole race. Your pace was perfect." Rachel and I laughed later, thinking that they had been watching our butts for thirty minutes!

After the race, we walked to the car and picked up Rachel's tote bag with our towels, Rachel's wrap, and our sunscreen. We walked to the clubhouse and got a table in the restaurant. Most people had something on in the restaurant. Rachel put on her mesh wrap, and I put on my towel. Sitting in a nice restaurant in just a towel felt funny. We had a nice breakfast, watching people coming and going in the clubhouse. Some were dressed, and some were not. I noticed two young women who had been in the race. They got a table out on the deck, just across from us. They both had put on bikini bottoms but were topless.

After breakfast we walked out to the pool and found two lounge chairs in the sun. The temperature still felt a little cool, and the sun felt good. Rachel sprayed sunscreen on my backside, and I did the same for her. We settled down for a few hours of naked sunning and people-watching.

The crowd at the pool was much more diverse than the race group. The average age was older, with many people in their forties and fifties. There also was more diversity in body types; not everyone was young or slender. Most people were quite tan all over, and again, almost everyone was shaved smooth. I looked over at Rachel, wondering what she was thinking, staring at so many naked men and their penises. There were big ones, little ones, straight ones, crooked ones, and even a pierced one. Yikes. I was sure she had never seen so many naked men in her entire life. Surprisingly, although the scene was unusual, it really wasn't that erotic. The book on naturism that we had read said that being nude was not about sex and that it was rare to see someone with an erection. I did not see anyone that way the entire day.

Rachel and I talked quietly, commenting on interesting people and the scene in general. "The people over there look like they all live here and know each other well," Rachel said.

"I thought so too," I said. "They also are all around the same age, late thirties, early forties. Do you think they are swingers? Everyone keeps hugging the attractive blonde woman. She looks like she enjoys being the center of attention."

We watched a middle-aged man dressed in tennis shorts going from group to group, stopping and chatting. He looked like a politician working the room. "He must be the mayor of Caliente," I said.

"He seems to know everyone, that's for sure," Rachel said. Later we saw him sitting with a few people on the side of the pool. The tennis shorts were gone.

In the afternoon we ordered margaritas. Our waitress from breakfast was now working the pool area as a cocktail waitress. We laughed that she now was topless. As it warmed up, we moved to a couple of chairs in the shade. An older couple came and sat in the chairs next to us. They reminded me of someone's grandma and grandpa, except that they took off their clothes and visited with us naked.

"Hi. How are you all doing?" the man asked.

"Doing great. It's a beautiful day," I replied.

"Did you run this morning?" the woman asked.

"Yes. It was really fun," Rachel answered.

"Your first time here then?" the woman asked Rachel.

"Yes, our first time. It's a beautiful resort. Do you live here?"

"Yes, we have a condo. We come down in the fall and stay through the spring. Then we go back to Michigan," the woman said. "This is our third year here."

We could have been chatting with them in any condo complex or mobile home park in Florida. The only difference was that we were all nude.

The crowd looked like mostly couples. There were a few single men, each of whom looked like an athlete or model. I wondered if they were there for show and to give the female patrons some eye candy to look at. All in all, Rachel and I felt comfortable in our skin. I thought Rachel looked great, and I was glad that we were both runners. Not bad for being fifty-something.

Rachel and I stayed until about four in the afternoon. As we walked to the car, it sounded like a band was warming up. We thought about staying for some music but decided that we had probably had enough stimulation for the day.

On the way back to Sarasota, I turned to Rachel. "Do you think you would do this again—the race next year or just a visit to the Caliente?"

Rachel thought for a few moments. "Yeah, I think so. It was pretty fun."

"I agree. This was pretty fun. But you know what?"

"What, Tim?"

"No one we know is going to believe we did this!"

"I think you're right about that. We'll probably never tell them anyway!"

We both laughed, and Rachel gave me a fist bump.

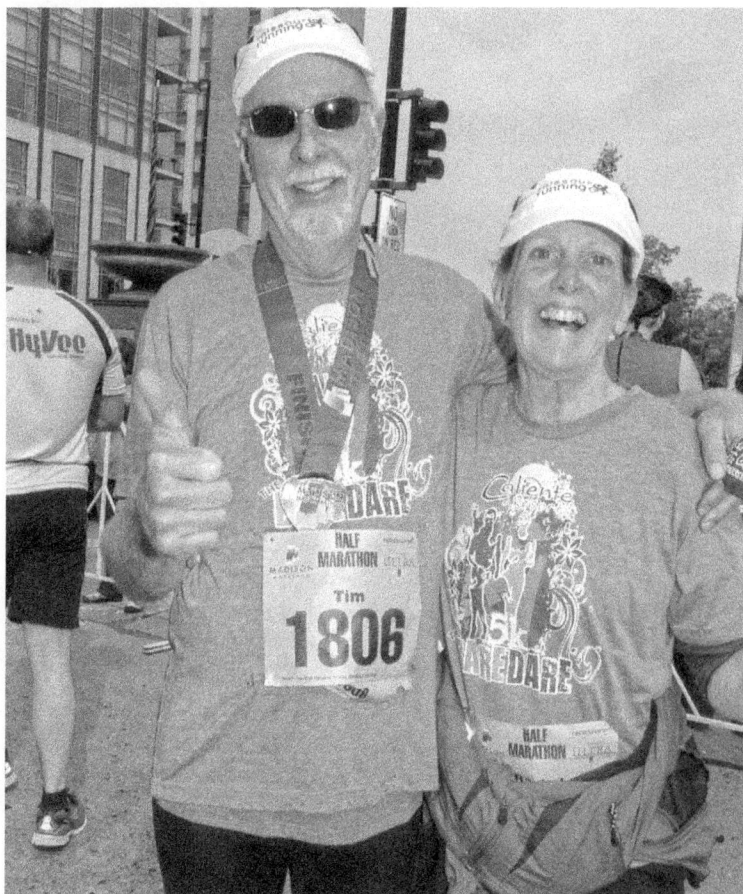

Celebrating the finish of the Madison Half Marathon and proudly wearing our Bare Dare tee-shirts, Madison, Wisconsin, 2013

16

A Mystery at the Inn

In the fall of 2014, Rachel and I took a two-week trip to New England, staying in country inns in Portsmouth and Holderness, New Hampshire. The Martin Hill Inn in Portsmouth was close to the Atlantic Ocean and Portsmouth's harbor. The Squam Lake Inn in Holderness was on Squam Lake, the setting for the movie *On Golden Pond* with Katharine Hepburn and Henry Fonda.

One evening I was reading the guest journal in our room, in which guests were invited to share their vacation experiences: restaurants they enjoyed, hikes that they went on, comments about the inn and innkeepers, or other observations. One entry was strikingly different from the others. I have changed the name and message just a little to protect the writer's privacy, but you will be able to understand her intention. Here is what it said:

> This is definitely my Year of Adventure. My husband
> of several years had an affair this past year. I mourned,
> cried, begged, and lost a bunch of weight. I even

tossed some of his clothes out the window, onto the front lawn. Now I am living in the now, as they say. I am on my first road trip. I'll see several parts of New Hampshire and Maine. I'm going to paint, hike, and eat and drink anything I want. This is my year. I can't wait to see what tomorrow may bring. Carpe diem!

—Annie from Wisconsin

I sat back, wishing that I could ask Annie a million questions. Did she dump her husband, or were they still together? How did she find out about the affair? Was she completely surprised? Did she know the other woman? How did her husband respond when she confronted him? Did she have family and friends to turn to for support? What were the things that helped her move on from this difficult experience? What did she end up doing on her road trip? Did she celebrate her newfound freedom or just try to drown her sorrows? Did she meet a handsome, unattached stranger at the inn who looked like George Clooney or Richard Gere? Why on earth did she choose to share something so personal with future guests at the inn? Was sharing her story somehow therapeutic for Annie?

I'll never know. But Rachel and I talked about Annie for quite a while that night and tried to imagine parts of her story. *Perhaps someday I'll write a travel tale about Annie from Wisconsin and fill in the missing pieces,* I decided.

PART 4
A Preview of Coming Attractions

Are you curious about Annie's story from the final travel tale, "A Mystery at the Inn"?
If you are, please enjoy this sneak peak of a new novel by Timothy Imhoff, *Painted Wings*.

Painted Wings

Chapter 1

Annie signed the paperwork for the man from the moving company and closed the door to her new apartment. She stood in the entrance hallway, looking at the piles and piles of unopened boxes, and began to feel overwhelmed. She felt tears forming in the corners of her eyes and wiped them away with the back of her hand. "Now don't get started, Annie Curtis," she said to herself. "You've been looking forward to this day for six months. This move represents complete separation from that SOB and an exciting new beginning."

Annie was thirty-eight years old and worked as an adjunct instructor at a large university in Madison, Wisconsin. She had a PhD in psychology and taught in the School of Education.

Shortly after the start of the fall semester, Annie had discovered that her husband was having an affair. Gary also worked at the university and was a tenured professor. It was the stereotypical affair between a mature professor and one of his graduate students. Annie and her husband had been married for twelve years, and the affair had come as a complete shock to her. Gary did not break off the affair when she discovered the tryst, but instead announced that he was in love with the young woman. The student even called Annie to introduce herself and say that she hoped they could all behave as adults and work out the life changes. "Who knows? One day we might become friends," the young woman had the audacity to tell Annie.

Annie was beside herself for a few weeks. She had discovered the affair upon finding a romantic greeting card in the pocket of one of Gary's suit jackets. She was so angry that she threw some of his clothes out onto the front lawn. He moved in with his new girlfriend, leaving Annie in the house near campus that they had owned for several years. After the initial shock, Annie experienced a short period of denial and begged her husband to move back home. He did not. She went through the various stages of grief and lost twenty-five pounds in the process—so at least there was a silver lining to this cloud.

With the help of a few close friends, Annie began to adjust to her new life. She hired a competent female attorney who specialized in helping women work through the divorce process. She and her husband agreed to sell their house and split all assets fifty-fifty. That would give Annie a small nest egg with which to begin her new life. Today was the beginning of that new life.

As Annie stared at the mountain of boxes, trying to figure out where to start, the doorbell rang. *My first houseguest,* Annie thought. She opened the door to find her best friend Monica standing on the doorstep, holding a large canvas grocery bag. Monica was a fellow instructor at the university and had been a big support during the last couple of months. Monica had gone through a similar life change a few years earlier when her husband died in a car accident. She had been coaching Annie in developing strategies for embracing change and building enthusiasm for new adventures. The two friends had spent many evenings at Monica's house, talking in front of the fire and sharing hopes, dreams, and fears. Monica was also one of those people who had a good book for every situation. She had shared several books with Annie about dealing with major life events and living more fully in the present. Monica was a few years younger than Annie, and Annie always felt sort of plain next to her and her dark brown eyes, silky auburn hair, and stylish wardrobe.

"Hey, girlfriend," Monica said as she gave Annie a hug. "Welcome to the neighborhood. I come bearing gifts."

"Thanks, sweetie. What did you bring?" Annie asked.

"Just the essentials for an unpacking party—wine and sushi, of course!"

"Sushi? I haven't had sushi in years. I don't even remember if I like it or not."

"I think it's one of the six or seven main food groups," Monica said, laughing. "Well, I know wine is in there somewhere for sure."

They put the sushi and wine in the refrigerator and began unpacking and setting up Annie's new apartment. After several hours, they had the bedroom set up, the kitchen unpacked, and almost all of the important stuff put away. "Let's take a break," Monica said.

"That sounds like a good idea. I'm starving. Even sushi is sounding pretty good."

They sat at the kitchen table and shared the first meal in Annie's new home.

"Okay, Annie," said Monica as they ate. "This was a big step. You've moved into your own place, and it suits you really well. Now the next step is doing something about your appearance."

Annie laughed. "What's wrong with my appearance?"

"Nothing's wrong with it. It's just a little too sixties—the long hair, all the denim and sweaters, the 'look, I'm a professor' glasses. Will you trust me to oversee your makeover, honey?"

Annie thought for a moment before answering. "Okay, I guess I trust you. Actually, I think that sounds fun. It's a great idea. But I think I better have some more wine!"

Monica made an appointment with her stylist the next weekend and accompanied Annie to the appointment. The stylist created a shorter, more contemporary look for Annie's light brown hair. She also added some blonde highlights. Annie laughed when she looked in the mirror at the salon and saw it. "Yikes, I look a bit androgynous, but I do like it!" Annie had never worn her hair so short before.

Annie traded in her rimless glasses for contact lenses and bought a pair of sleek, designer sunglasses to shade her pretty brown eyes. Having lost twenty-five pounds did not hurt, either. She had always been fit, but dropping the pounds made her feel more attractive. She decided to take things to the next level. Annie had been a runner as a young woman and had even enjoyed running in 5K and 10K races. She bought a book on preparing for half marathons and got a subscription to *Runner's World* magazine. Annie started running in the mornings and followed the recommended schedules for distance and speed. Sometimes she ran in the park, sometimes through the neighborhood streets, and when the weather was bad, at the university indoor track. Her goal was to be ready to try her first half marathon in six months.

Because of her weight loss and improving muscle tone, Annie soon needed to replace some clothes that no longer fit. She really liked her new running outfits and how she looked in her shorts, running skirts, running tights, and sports bras. Annie began wearing more leggings, shorter skirts, sleeveless tops, and jackets. Her friends were excited about her new look, and she noticed that both students and faculty seemed to be checking her out sometimes. Of course, Monica took total credit for the makeover.

Some of the stranger experiences during this time were the awkward attempts at dating and meeting new people. Many of her female friends were one half of couples that Annie and her husband had socialized with. The invites from most of these couples reduced to a trickle over time. Then there were the awkward dinner parties. Annie would arrive to find an unattached single man as the only other invited guest. At the end of the evening, the host would look expectantly at Annie, hoping that she and the other guest would arrange another meeting.

Annie tried an online dating site briefly but found the experience too complicated and somewhat stressful. Once she made her profile public, she seemed to always be juggling a few different potential matches simultaneously. But after her experience with her husband cheating on her, Annie found that she did not enjoy interacting with multiple men at the same time. It was hard to keep track of what she had already said to each person. Most of the dates that she went on were similar. It seemed like many of the men were professional daters. They talked about why they were single—it was always the ex's fault—and they talked about their funny or disastrous online dates. Annie wondered how they would describe her to their next date or the one after that.

One of the online dating traditions with which she was most uncomfortable was the supposed "three-date rule." One of her dates explained over dinner that the rule of thumb for online dating was that if a couple made it to the third date, it was expected that they would have sex. After all, they needed to find out whether they were compatible. Annie just smiled sweetly and replied that she had never liked following rules.

Meanwhile, Annie grew to like the diversity of her new neighborhood, the mixture of people, and the somewhat funky vibe. There were lots of small, independent shops, coffee houses, and restaurants within walking distance of her second-floor apartment on Monroe Street. It was close to the university arboretum and the Henry Vilas Zoo.

As an adjunct instructor at the university, Annie taught on a semester-by-semester contract. In past years she had taught one summer class, but this year she decided to take the summer off. Monica had labeled this Annie's "Year of Adventure," and a summer road trip sounded like a good way to kick it off.

One evening in April, after dinner with Monica, Annie pulled out an atlas and spread it open on the kitchen table. "Where should I go?" Annie asked. "My only limitations are time and money." As she looked at the US map, her gaze kept returning to New England. As a teenager, Annie had spent several summer vacations in New Hampshire and Maine. Her aunt Jane lived in a lovely country house, just outside of Bar Harbor. Annie exchanged e-mails with her from time to time but had not visited in many years.

"Maybe New England would be good," Annie said. "My aunt Jane lives in Maine, not far from the coast. I wouldn't want to spend the entire summer with her, but perhaps we would enjoy a week or so together. I could build my adventure around several different places in New Hampshire and Maine. I could hike in the White Mountains, eat lobster in Portsmouth and Portland, and paint landscapes along the Maine coast. I haven't gotten out my paints in so long."

"That sounds like the perfect trip!" Monica said. "You will have some family time, but more importantly, some time to spread your wings and look for new experiences. Who knows? You might meet a mysterious stranger and find your passionate side again!"

"I'd settle for a few weeks of rest and relaxation, I think."

Monica looked at Annie with a mischievous sparkle in her eyes. "This is your year, Annie. Be open to new experiences, of all kinds!"

Classes for the spring semester ended in mid-May. On a sunny morning at the beginning of June, Annie's Subaru wagon was loaded, and she pulled out of the parking lot of her apartment. She looked up at her apartment window. "See you in August," she said aloud. Annie felt her pulse quicken as she pulled away. I'm really doing this! she thought. Who knows what the summer has in store for me?

Painted Wings

Chapter 2

It had been a few years since Annie had done a road trip of any distance. She did not intend to make any stops on the way east other than for meals and a motel. The route outlined by her navigation system would take her to Detroit and then across the border into Canada. She would travel near Toronto and Montreal, before heading south through Vermont and New Hampshire. Her plan was to drive until early evening and then look for a motel off the highway, near a real restaurant, which meant someplace that had more than fried food and that had a good glass of wine.

Annie had always enjoyed driving and quickly got into the rhythm of the road. She had signed up for XM Radio before she left and had a wonderful variety of classic rock music to listen to. She even had the Grateful Dead Channel. Annie made it to the outskirts of Toronto a little after seven o'clock in the evening, after just over eleven hours on the road. She found a nice motel, and the woman at the reception desk recommended a restaurant a few miles away that was known for its seafood offerings. Annie enjoyed her broiled sea bass and a glass of chardonnay from Ontario.

The next morning, she started off early again. Annie's first destination was Portsmouth, New Hampshire. She had made reservations for a week at the Cranberry Inn, in the heart of town. Located on the Atlantic Ocean and boasting a working port, Portsmouth was one of New Hampshire's largest cities, though it still was not very large. The downtown area was busy and filled with places to shop, eat, listen to music, and people-watch. Portsmouth wasn't far from the University of New Hampshire in Durham and had the feel of a university community.

Upon arriving, Annie parked her car behind the Cranberry Inn and found the entrance. The inn was a large older home on one of the main downtown streets. It had beautifully landscaped gardens and ten guest rooms spread between two buildings. Annie entered through the front door and found an antique bell on a wooden stand near the entryway and a reception desk facing the door. Annie rang the bell and waited just a minute before a man walked out from the dining room.

He greeted her with a smile. "Good afternoon, miss. I'm Bill Martin, one of the innkeepers. Welcome to the Cranberry Inn!"

Bill looked to be in his early sixties. He had white hair and a trim white beard, and he reminded Annie of a slimmed-down version of Ernest Hemingway.

"Hi, Bill. I'm Annie. Annie Curtis."

"Is this your first trip to Portsmouth, Annie?"

"I've been here before, but it's been several years."

"Well, welcome back then. You'll be in the Mountain Laurel Room on the second floor. You'll need to climb a few steps, but you are rewarded with a nice view."

"Steps are fine. I can use the workout."

Bill nodded. "Breakfast is served between seven thirty and eight thirty here in the main dining room. Let me know if you have any strong likes, dislikes, or allergies. Do you drink regular or decaf coffee? Knowing helps me have everything ready for our guests."

"Regular coffee will be great. And I'll eat most anything for breakfast."

"That's perfect. We are walking distance to most all of downtown from here. You will find a wonderful variety of restaurants, and all are good. The ones that aren't good don't last very long."

"I'm looking forward to exploring Portsmouth," Annie said. "I may go into Portland too."

"Kittery, Maine, is just across the bridge, and Portland is a bit further north. Let me know if you want any recommendations. You can help yourself to anything you find in the dining room during your stay. We usually have a little happy hour with wine and cheese between five and six each evening. Feel free to join us."

"Thanks, Bill. I just might do that."

Bill handed Annie the key to her room. "Welcome to Portsmouth, Annie! Let me know if I can do anything to make your stay more enjoyable."

Annie got her suitcase and laptop computer bag from the car and carried them up to her room. The Mountain Laurel Room was bright and elegantly decorated with antique furnishings. A pretty quilt covered the queen-size bed. French doors opened onto a small balcony, looking over the gardens and parts of downtown Portsmouth. Annie unpacked her suitcase and hung up a few things. *This will do just fine,* Annie thought. She again felt her pulse racing. *I can do anything I want!*

After so many hours in the car, Annie felt like a run would be good. It was late afternoon and too early for dinner. She changed into black running shorts and a black running bra with a bright orange design resembling flames. This was one of her favorite running outfits, and it showed off the progress she was making toning the muscles in her legs, arms, and belly. She laced up her running shoes and headed down the stairs and outside. As Annie ran toward the harbor, she stayed on the sidewalks; they weren't crowded. She passed a few other runners, nodding to them as she passed. It seemed like no matter where they were, runners formed a friendly community. Annie ran until she reached Prescott Park, a decent-sized city park that ran along the water. From the park she could see the harbor, and Annie watched a large ship slowly make its way in from the ocean.

By the time she made it back to the inn, Annie estimated that she had done about a four-mile run. Her legs felt good as she stretched out in the garden beside the parking area. When she was done, she went to her room and took a relaxing shower. As she stood in her room drying off after the shower, she wondered, *What next?*

"I think it's a good evening to explore the town. And I'm getting hungry," she said aloud to herself. Annie put on a pair of black leggings, a purple batik-print dress, and black half boots. Her new, shorter hair style did not require much attention to look sassy. She put on a little lip gloss and was ready to go.

Annie walked back down toward the harbor and explored several of the side streets. The sidewalks were more crowded now with people meeting after work or going out for dinner. She passed a few seafood restaurants with seating on the water and picked one. The friendly young hostess—Jen according to her name badge—escorted her out to the back deck to a small table overlooking the harbor.

"I really like your dress and leggings," Jen said. "The color looks great on you."

Annie smiled. "Thanks, Jen."

The large ship that Annie had seen while running was now moored at the dock, and giant cranes were unloading what looked like sand into large piles on the shore. "That's salt," Jen told her. "It's the salt that will be used on the roads this winter all over New Hampshire and Maine. It comes into Portsmouth all the way from South America."

"That's amazing," Annie replied. "I never would have imagined."

"Yeah, it's pretty cool! Enjoy your meal," Jen said and moved back to her station.

Annie had been looking forward to a lobster dinner, a guilty pleasure, for as long as she had been planning the trip. She opted for a lobster roll when the server arrived to take her order and was not disappointed. Large chunks of lobster meat with just a hint of lemon rested on a toasted hot dog roll. The dinner came with fries and coleslaw, and Annie enjoyed a nice glass of chardonnay with the meal.

As she stared out at the harbor, enjoying her first real New England meal in years, Annie had a sudden feeling of sadness. The moment was just about perfect, but she was sitting all alone. She looked around the deck at the other diners. She was the only one flying solo.

For most of the months after the separation, Annie had refused to go out by herself. Sitting at a restaurant alone with just her Kindle to keep her company didn't feel right. She was comfortable at coffee shops, though, and she didn't mind going to movies by herself because when the theater lights went down, she always felt part of a group.

You can do this, Annie, she told herself. *You are a strong person and an attractive woman. You are in a cool city at the beginning of an exciting adventure.* Annie took the last sip of wine from her glass. She smiled at her passing waitress and pointed at her glass. "I think I'll have another."

Annie watched the activity around the harbor and on the deck as she enjoyed her wine. She gradually relaxed and smiled to herself as she thought about how far she had come in the past few months. After she settled her bill, she left the restaurant and continued to explore the streets around the harbor. She passed the entrance to Strawberry Bank, a several-block neighborhood of restored homes that had been turned into an urban museum of sorts. *Maybe I'll check that out tomorrow,* she thought.

A little while later, Annie came to an unusual storefront. Above the door was a weathered, hand-carved wooden sign: "The Bookstore." From the outside, it looked like a coffee shop or campus hangout, with posters advertising upcoming entertainment. Annie walked in and saw that the Bookstore was just that and more. Several rooms were filled with bookshelves, like a normal bookstore. Signs indicated the content of the different shelves: poetry, literature, movies, children's books, and many other categories. Some books looked new, and others, gently used. Tables, sofas, and chairs were scattered throughout the rooms as well. At some tables students were studying and looked like they had been camped out for hours. At other tables people looked like they were eating dinner. There was a bar along one wall with chalkboards listing wines, craft beers, sandwiches, and other snacks. It looked like some patrons were ordering at the bar, and others had waitstaff serving them at their tables. The rooms were not crowded, but a wide variety of people were enjoying the evening. Annie got the impression that most patrons probably lived or worked in the neighborhood. Many of them seemed to know each other. There were lots of interesting tattoos and piercings.

What an interesting place! she thought. Annie found a stool at the bar and watched as the young bohemian-looking woman behind the bar poured draft beers and served a few other customers. She looked like she was in her early thirties and had long blonde hair and a slender build. She wore faded jeans, a dark blue tank top, and several handwoven bracelets on each wrist. She had some striking body art on her arms, and Annie could see that she had more on her back. She moved with ease behind the bar, not rushing, but working very efficiently. Finally, she came over to Annie and smiled. She had a pretty smile and blue eyes.

"Hi, I'm Katie. Welcome to the Bookstore! What can I get you tonight?"

"Do you have a chardonnay by the glass?"

"Sure. Actually, several. What kind of chardonnay do you usually like?"

"I like it more on the dry side and not too oaky."

"Then I'd recommend the Naked Lady. It's made in New York State and is unoaked. I think it's crisp and delicious."

"It sounds like you know your wine, Katie. I'll try a Naked Lady then," Annie said, and they both laughed.

"What's your name?" Katie asked.

"It's Annie."

Katie held out her hand. "It's nice to meet you, Annie!"

Annie felt a bit awkward but shook Katie's hand. She could not remember another bartender greeting her in a similar way. She tried to not grip Katie's hand too lightly or too hard. Finally, she just relaxed and laughed again.

"This is a really cool place. Have you worked here long?"

www.ingramcontent.com/pod-product-compliance
Lightning Source LLC
Chambersburg PA
CBHW032111040426
42337CB00040B/189